GREAT DANES

PAST AND PRESENT

Photo., Sport and General.

MISS BETTY RANK, WITH JAVAR OF OUBOROUGH, PAMPA OF OUBOROUGH, PLAZA OF OUBOROUGH, AND PRIDE OF OUBOROUGH.

GREAT DANES

Past and Present

By the late
Dr Morell Mackenzie

2nd Editon
Revised and brought up to date by
Arthur F Marples

Vintage Dog Books
Home Farm
44 Evesham Road
Cookhill, Alcester
Warwickshire
B49 5LJ

www.vintagedogbooks.com

ISBN 978-1-84664-074-2 (paperback)
ISBN 978-1-84664-075-9 (hardback)

Published by Vintage Dog Books 2006
Vintage Dog Books is an imprint of Read Books

British Library Cataloguing-in-Publication Data
A catalogue record for this book is available
from the British Library.

Vintage Dog Books
Home Farm
44 Evesham Road
Cookhill, Alcester
Warwickshire
B49 5LJ

GREAT DANES,

—PAST AND PRESENT—

BY THE LATE
Dr. MORELL MACKENZIE.

With an Additional Chapter on Veterinary Diseases by
A. Cornish Bowden, M.R.C.V.S.

2nd EDITION
Revised aud brought up to date by Arthur F. Marples,
Sub-Editor of " Our Dogs."

———————

" Oh, that mine enemy would write a book."

———————

" I have gathered a posie of other men's
flowers, and nothing but the thread that binds
them is mine own."

∴

MANCHESTER :
" OUR DOGS " PUBLISHING COMPANY, LIMITED,
" OUR DOGS " BUILDINGS, OXFORD ROAD STATION APPROACH.

Index to Chapters.

Index to Illustrations.

PREFACE.

In presenting the following pages to the public I trust that it will not be thought that I do so with any idea of having a special claim to being more competent than other lovers of the breed. No one can write a book without being seriously impressed by his own limited capabilities and shortcomings.

My only excuse for this book is that there is no other ; and as everyone with any experience has refused, I am hoping that my knowledge and experience, little as they are, may be better than none at all, and may be some help to beginners.

I have one advantage for the work, and that is the number of my friends : for I am well aware that the chief value of this book, if there is any, is contained in the advice that has been given me by them. Although they would not perpetrate so serious a crime as the writing of a book, they are yet guilty of being accessories before the deed, and have been kind enough to give me an immense amount of valuable information. What I should have done without them I hesitate to think, and while it is quite true that too many cooks spoil the broth, there has in the present case been only one culinary preceptor, and I have only used those ingredients which thirty years' experience has taught me to be really valuable.

To Dr. Sidney Turner and Mr. R. E. Nicholas I am indeed indebted, not only for the careful way in which they have corrected proofs, but for their constant advice and experience, which probably surpass those of any other canine authorities. Mr. Alfred Walker, of Lytham, and Dr. Osburne have also been exceedingly kind in the help they have given me, not only in doggy matters, but on many other points.

It would be difficult for me to sufficiently thank Mr. Cornish Bowden, not only for the chapter that he has so kindly written, but also for the experiments he has performed, dissections he has undertaken, and careful notes which he has compiled with a view of assisting in this book, and for which he will get no credit but the poor thanks I now offer him.

Mr. Nicholas was originally to have written the two chapters on Food and Feeding, and if he had only been able to do so I should have been very glad, while it would have added to the interest of the book. Although he was prevented by illness from doing what I wanted, Mr. Nicholas was good enough to place all that he had written at my disposal. The chapters on Feeding are really the views of Mr. Nicholas, and where I differ from him I have made a point of saying so definitely.

In conclusion, besides the gentlemen I have mentioned, I must thank Mr. Sheaf for the beautiful photographs he has allowed me to use as headpieces ; and the Duke of Marlborough for permitting me to have a drawing made of the tapestry at Blenheim, and Mr. S. Dadd for so kindly executing it. I am also greatly obliged to Mr. Blass for the photograph of the plan he advocates in feeding puppies, and the numerous ladies and gentlemen who have so kindly allowed illustrations of their dogs to appear.

There are many people for whom the only attraction in the book will be the illustrations. There are many who believe that they have only to buy a couple of champions and they are competent to judge the following year. I can assure them that the longer they live the more they will be impressed by their own ignorance of Great Danes, and it is only now, thirty-two years to the day since I had my first Dane, that I am beginning to hope I have learned something.

MORELL MACKENZIE.

PREFACE TO NEW EDITION.

As a greatly reawakened interest is evident in the Great Dane fancy, an up-to-date and revised edition is now presented of this well known and popular book on the breed originally written by that eminent expert, the late Dr. Morell Mackenzie.

The new edition contains all the salient and interesting historical features of the old volume, with the addition of articles and statistics bringing it up to present-day requirements. Embellished as it is with photographs of celebrated past and present specimens of the breed, it will no doubt prove a useful addition to every " Daneite's " library.

A. F. M.

Great Danes, Past and Present.

CHAPTER 1.

History.

Any attempt to give the actual origin of the Great Dane must be purely speculative and theoretical. If we take, first of all, what I might call a bird's eye view of the subject we can trace the breed back with certainty for many hundred years, as it undoubtedly existed on the Continent in the Middle Ages. Earlier than this, the Saxons hunted the wild boar in the forests of England before the Norman Conquest with dogs resembling the Great Dane, and, as Alaunts, the descendants of these dogs are to be found in pictures and tapestries of hunting scenes of the 14th and 15th centuries, just as the paintings of Snyder and Teniers, and the prints of Ridlinger, give the most lifelike representations of the Great Dane in the Middle Ages of the Continent.

Some historians believe the Great Dane to be the true descendant of the Molossian dog—the ancestor of the Mastiff—on account of his resemblance to the Molossus shown in Roman and Grecian statuary, and there is no doubt that the old type of Great Dane was by no means unlike the Mastiff, while a supposed proof of the breed's great antiquity is a Grecian coin in the Royal Museum at Munich, which dates from the 5th century B.C., and represents a dog which much resembles the Great Dane of to-day.

1

Lastly, we have writers who consider the great antiquity of this breed as proved from the fact that a dog sufficiently similar to be considered his ancestor is depicted on some of the oldest Egyptian monuments, supposed to date from about 3000 B.C.*

As far as I can find out, the Great Dane seems to have existed continuously from the earliest times in these islands. There has been great confusion between the Irish Wolfhound and the Great Dane, but there can be no doubt that the two breeds existed side by side (though they were crossed indiscriminately), and it is difficult to know to which breed some of the earlier writers are referring when they talk of the Irish Greyhound. Richardson† tells us that Pliny relates a combat in which the dogs of Epirus bore a part ; he describes them as much taller than Mastiffs and of Greyhound form, detailing an account of their contest with a lion and an elephant. This, he thinks, establishes the identity of the Great Dane with the dogs of Epirus.

Richardson was evidently well acquainted with the breed, which he describes as rarely standing " less than 30in. at the shoulder, and usually more." He describes a Great Dane belonging to the Duke of Buccleuch, which at 18 years measured 32in., and which he considered must have measured at least 32½in. in its prime.

Strabo writes of a large and powerful Greyhound in use among the Celtic and Pictic nations, which was held in such high estimation by them as to have been imported into Gaul for the purposes of the chase. A picture is very vivid in my imagination, though exactly where I have seen it I cannot now call to my mind : it depicted a Viking in his ship, under full sail, with a blue Great Dane standing in the bows.

Silius describes a large and powerful Greyhound as having being imported into Ireland by the Belgæ, thus identifying it with the celebrated Belgic dog.

As I have already said, it is extremely difficult to decide as to which breed the above remarks refer, and each reader will probably hold his own view ; but personally I should be inclined to think it was the Irish Wolfhound

* Cassel's " Book of the Dog," Vol. I., P. 4.
† " Book of the Dog," by Vero Shaw (see Irish Wolfhound).

and not the Great Dane, as the former's rough coat would be of the greater defensive value. Whichever view we accept does not affect the antiquity of the breed, while the constant appearance of a Great Dane in Snyder's, Rubens', and, in my opinion, Paulo Veronese's paintings (where the dog frequently resembles the Great Dane as portrayed by Buffon) is convincing testimony of its popularity in the Middle Ages.

Some years ago the *Badminton Magazine* published a series of "Old Sporting Prints," some of which contained excellent representations of the Great Dane. In the November number for 1895 there is an illustration of Boarhounds from an etching by Antonio Tempesta, copied by him in 1609 from an old tapestry. In the February number of 1896 there is also a picture of five Hounds attacking a wild boar. One of these—a black dog—is really an admirable representation of the modern Great Dane.

Other writers who mention this dog are Camden (1568); Holinshed (1560) ; Ware (1654) ; Evelyn (1660-1670), who describes it as "a stately creature indeed, and did beat a cruel Mastiff"; Ray (1697), who says it is "the greatest dog I have ever seen"; and Goldsmith, who, writing in 1770, says of the great Irish Wolfhound, "I have seen about a dozen, the largest of these was about four feet high, as tall as a calf of a year old. He was made extremely like a Greyhound, but more robust, and inclining to the figure of the French Matin or Great Dane."

Cuvier gives the origin of our breed as the Matin's, the anatomical characteristic of which was a more or less elongated head with the parietal or side bones of the head gradually drawing towards each other, but Buffon makes it spring from the Irish Greyhound, which he derives from a cross between the original Shepherd dog and the Mastiff.

The latter authority says* that the Matin exported to the North became the Great Danish dog, and when acclima-

---

* *Oeuvres de Leclere* Tome. 4 rieme, p. 64. Le matin transporte au Nord est devenu Grand Danois et transporté au midi est devenu levrier. Le dogue transporté d'Angleterre en Danemark est devenu petit Danois et ce meme petit Danois transporté dans les climats chauds est devenu chien Turc. Le Grand Danois transporté en Irelande, en Ukraine; en Tartarie, en Epire, en Albanie est devenu chien d'Irlande et c'est le plus grand, de tous les chiens. Toutes ces races avec leur varietés n'ont été produites que par l'influence du climat, jointe à la douceur de l'abri à l'effet de la nourriture et au resultat d'une education soign'ee.

tised in Ireland, the Ukraine, Tartary, Epirus and Albania, developed into the Great Wolf dog known by the name of the Irish Wolfhound.

I think that I have now mentioned all the earlier writers, and there remain those historians who have written within the memory of living men or their immediate predecessors. From their accounts there can be no possible doubt that the Great Dane has existed in England and Ireland for the last 150 years, that it has been always known by that name, and that it is not, as many people would have us believe, a new breed to England, introduced after the Franco-German war, though it cannot be denied that the breed has been vastly benefited by the great pains which were taken in Germany to improve it, and by the number of good dogs which were at that time imported into England.

In 1794 certain dogs belonging to the then Lord Altamont were put forward as being Irish Wolfhounds, but there can be no doubt that they were nothing of the sort, for in the third volume of the Transactions of the Linnæan Society, Mr. Lambert, in describing these dogs, gives a very fair description of the Great Dane, and specially mentions that "their hair was short and smooth, and their colour brown-and-white or black-and-white."

In the "Sportsman's Cabinet," a very rare book, published in 1803, of which only a limited number of copies were issued, the writer says: "The Irish Greyhound is a very ancient race; they are much larger than the Mastiff, exceedingly ferocious." He then proceeds to give a most admirable description of a modern Great Dane. It is, however, illustrated by Reinagle with a picture of the Irish Wolfhound. Whether the letterpress or the print is in the wrong place is not really material, as it shows that the Great Dane existed in England at that time.

About the year 1800,* Sydenham Edwards wrote his "Cynographia Brittanica," and this book clears up any possible doubt as to the Great Dane being at that time, at all events, a naturalised British subject. There is a picture of three Great Danes which could not be mistaken, though the brindle dog, which is standing up, is rather weak in the

* "Cynographia Brittanica," by Sydenham Edwards, 1800.

4

GREAT DANE. SKETCHED FROM TAPESTRY IN 3RD STATE ROOM, BLENHEIM PALACE.

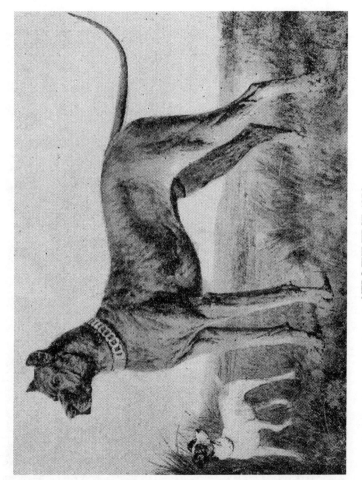

NERO THE FIRST, 1876.

muzzle, and the way his tail is carried hardly conforms with the rules as laid down by the Great Dane Club. The other two members of the "team" are a Harlequin and a Merle, each lying down, and the Harlequin, which is in the foreground, is in most respects quite typical. In height Edwards describes them as 28 to 31 inches, and in form between a Greyhound and a Mastiff. He goes on to say that the "head is straight, muzzle rather pointed, ears short, half pendulous (often cropped), eyes in some white, in others half-white or yellow, chest deep, belly small, legs straight and strong, tail thin and wiry, in some curled over, in others straight."

Further interesting comments of Sydenham Edwards are :—

"Colour sandy red or pale yellow, with often a blaze of white on the face."

"A beautiful variety, called the Harlequin Dane, has a finely marbled coat with large and small spots of black, grey, liver colour, or sandy red, upon a white ground."

"The grand figure, bold muscular action, and elegant carriage, would recommend him to notice had he no useful properties."

"Not noisy, but of approved dignity becoming his intrepid character, he keeps his state in silence. That he is obliged to be muzzled to prevent his attacking his own species or other domestic animals adds much to the effect, as it supposes power and gives an idea of protection."

"The common coach dog is an humble attendant of the servants and horses : the Dane appears the escort of his lord, bold and ready in his defence. I certainly think no equipage can have arrived at its acme of grandeur until a couple of Harlequin dogs precede the pomp."

"He must be kept in subjection, as he attacks sheep with deadly fury."

Lastly, Edwards remarks that he does not know at what time the breed was introduced into England, and that Lord Cadogan's Dane "figured in the tapestry of the Siege of Bochain at Blenheim, who attended his master in all the actions of the gallant Marlborough."*

* See Illustration page i.

5

E. Jesse, in 1846, writes of the Harlequin that its "colour is generally white, marked all over his body with black spots and patches, in general larger than those of the Dalmatian. Ears are for most part white, while the Dalmatian's are black."

Coming to 1857, we hear of a Great Dane, Prince, which belonged to Mr. Francis Butler, of New York, and was brought to England, while Rawdon Lee has a note of a black-and-white Great Dane, belonging to Sir Roger Palmer, in 1863 or 1864.

This shows that the name of Great Dane, as well as the breed, was already well known in England at the time of its reintroduction (if I may so call it) from the Continent about 1876 and 1877. There can be no doubt, however, that the excellence of the present-day Great Dane in England is largely owing to the importation of Continental dogs and the great care and attention bestowed abroad on breeding up to a definite standard, and for certain well-defined points, can never be over-estimated.

I have already mentioned that there has for a long time existed on the Continent a breed of big, powerfully built dogs which were used for the chase and as guards of the home. They were usually cropped, of a blue or black-and-white colour, and in general appearance resembled the Great Dane. These, from the fact that they were largely used for boar-hunting in the days antecedent to gunpowder, were known as Hatzruden; other varieties of the big Continental dog were called Saufanger, Ulmer Dogge, and Rottweiler Metzerghund. They differed from each other in various small points, and were, I think, distinct from the Great Dane as known in England at that time. In the various parts of Germany the dogs had different characteristics, but there were two chief divisions—namely, a strong, heavy dog which belonged to the Northern part of Germany, and a much lighter dog that belonged to the Southern and hilly part. These two distinctions remain to-day, and it will be noticed that the Northern dog, in addition to being much heavier, has much more life, much more "go" in him, and is much less timid, than the Southern dog, which is built on more elegant lines and is generally of a somewhat nervous disposition.

After the war of 1870, when the whole of Germany was throbbing with martial ardour and patriotism, it occurred to the German dog lovers to choose a national and emblematic dog, and they fixed on this big, powerful variety, christening him the " Deutsche Dogge." It is from these dogs, crossed with the English Great Dane, that the modern English Great Dane has sprung. In those days each individual in Germany who owned a Deutsche Dogge considered him the ideal type, but it was only after constant interchange of dogs and ideas between the different cities, by careful consideration of the good and bad points of the different types, by special attention given to remove coarseness in head, tail and coat, and by constant painstaking and care, that the Germans finally fixed on a definite type which they considered satisfactory. All parts of Germany gave their help and added their quota, and the very greatest credit is due to them for having evolved from the coarse, powerful and somewhat ungainly dogs of the middle of the last century, the superb animal described by Mr. Cooper as the Apollo Belvidere of dogdom.

To show what has been done one need only compare the photograph of Rolf the First,* a big winner at the Berlin Show of 1883, with one of the modern champions.

The Deutsche Doggen Klub, the first German specialist club, was formed in 1888, but the Great Dane Club was founded in England in 1882. In 1903 the Northern Great Dane Club was formed, and these two, working hand in hand, did more than anything else to promote the interests and increase the popularity of the Great Dane in this country.

Before concluding the History of the breed it may be as well to mention briefly the views that were held in Germany about 1880.

Herr Gustav Lang, of Stuttgart,† writing to Mr. Vero Shaw, says: " The German breeders had determined to classify the Boarhound, Ulmer Dog, and Great Dane as one breed, which they proposed to call the German Mastiff. The distinctions between these various breeds were, if any, so slight that mischief was being done by any attempts to dissociate them. In fact, it was almost impossible to do so. Even if

* See Illustration page iii.
†" Book of the Dog," by Vero Shaw, 1884.

7

originally distinct, the slight differences of type had become obliterated."

Again, writing of the Harlequin or "Tiger" dog, he says : "The 'Tiger' dog only differs from the German Mastiff in colour. It is peculiar that we in Germany by 'Tiger' do not mean the colour of a tiger, but like a 'tiger' horse, for example, which is white with small dark spots, as distinguished from the piebald horse."

Again, he says : "About sixty years ago these dogs were much in fashion. They subsequently became very scarce, so that it was thought they had died out." In Vero Shaw's book, which was published in 1884, there is an excellent picture, a woodcut of Herr Wuster's "Tiger German Mastiff" Flora. This is a very good Harlequin, and would do credit to any kennel at the present time.

Another German correspondent of Vero Shaw's was Herr R. von Schmiedeberg, at that time editor of "Der Hund," who wrote : "Some years ago we still had the Ulmer Doggen, Hatzruden Danische Doggen, etc., but it has been impossible to settle with any clearness whether they were separate races. The Ulmer Doggen received their name in consequence of the very large Tiger Doggen having become so rare. The colour of the German dog is quite a matter of taste, but those of one colour, without any white marks, are mostly preferred."

Herr Schmiedeberg gave the following description of the dog at this time : "Figure high, elegant ; head rather long ; nose of medium length, thick, not pointed ; lower jaw to project only a little ; point of nose large, black, except with Tiger dogs, where the same may be flesh-coloured or spotted ; lip trifle overhanging ; ears placed high and pointed ; eyes brown, not too light (except with Tiger dogs, which often have glassy eyes) ; earnest and sharp look ; neck pretty long and strong, without dewlap ; chest broad and deep ; back long and straight ; toes closed, nails strong and long ; thigh bone muscular ; knees deep, almost like a Greyhound ; tail not too long, hardly to reach the hocks and to be carried almost in a straight line with the back, never to be curly ; the coat of the whole body, and particularly the tail, to be short and smooth ; back claws are allowed on the hind feet

8

if they are firm and not loose ; colour bright-black, wavy, yellow, blue, if possible without any marks, or if striped usually with glassy eyes."

It will be noted that in the standard given by Herr von Schmiedeberg, which is probably one of the earliest drawn up in Germany, great stress is laid on the dewclaws only being allowed if they are firm and not loose. This is because the dewclaws are supposed to show a St. Bernard cross. There can be no doubt that St. Bernards were largely crossed with Great Danes at the beginning of the last century, on account of the threatened extinction of St. Bernards—any St. Bernard fancier knows this,—and I have no doubt that (until quite recently on the Continent) the crossing has continued to get the pure white in the Harlequins.

The progress made by this breed in the last fifty years, is truly wonderful when one considers the exceptional difficulties with which it has had to contend. In the first place the Quarantine Act forbidding the landing of dogs in this country, unless detained for six months at a place supervised by a Veterinary Surgeon appointed or sanctioned by the Board of Agriculture and Fisheries, was a severe blow. It made the importation of dogs, which means fresh blood, an expensive amusement, and one that could consequently be indulged in only by comparatively rich people or dealers. It thus diminished our supply of fresh blood, and tended to promote excessive in-breeding.

The second severe blow received by the fancy was the passing of the Kennel Club's law, on February 27th, 1895, which forbade cropping. Our late King Edward felt strongly on the subject, and a letter of his to Mr. Farman undoubtedly had great influence in causing legislation. Though cropping is to be generally condemned on humane grounds, it must be admitted that, paradoxical as it may appear, it is sometimes the kindest thing to do, an excitable, high-spirited, and active dog often damaging its ears so severely by continued shaking and knocking that cropping or amputation is the only possible remedy. There can be no doubt that the long, untouched ears greatly detract from the dog's alert, lively and keen appearance, while they largely alter the graceful neck which should be such a marked characteristic.

It is quite certain that when cropping was stopped a large number of fanciers gave up the breed altogether and that for five or six years the breed so languished as to suggest that it would never regain its popularity in England.

In conclusion, it should be mentioned that the Great Dane is placed among the non-sporting breeds by the Kennel Club, to the great dissatisfaction of many fanciers who strongly urge its claims as a sporting dog.

They were originally considered sporting dogs, but were afterwards relegated to the non-sporting division. Hence great confusion arose in 1895, as while registered as "non-sporting" they were allowed to compete and win at Manchester and also at Olympia as "sporting dogs." Mr. Theo : Marples and the Hon. Secretary of the Great Dane Club, together with other people, took a great deal of interest in the matter, and finally Dr. Sidney Turner gave notice that at the next meeting of the Kennel Club Committee he would move " that Great Danes henceforward be classed as sporting dogs." Mr. G. W. Hickman strongly opposed Dr. Turner, and in reply to the latter's remark that " surely the name of Boarhound was not given without reason," pointed out, as he had already done some time previously, that the name Boarhound was simply a corruption of the German word *bauerhund* (farm-dog), which was the name it was known by some years previously. In proof of this he cited the following passage from Col. Hamilton Smith's work on the dog in Jardine's Naturalists' Library.* In referring to the group of watch dogs, under which head he classified Great Danes, Col. Smith remarks : " It is in this tribe that some of the largest and finest dogs of antiquity should be sought, and where the southern nations have found their *matin*, which the English have improperly transferred to our original great Bull-dog by altering into Mastiff, and the German's name Bauerhund or farm dog." Mr. Hickman also added that while the Great Dane was capable of being used for sporting purposes, in classification, the primary object for which a dog was kept must be alone considered, and in this case it was as a farm dog. It will be noticed that this view is opposed to the theory that the Great Dane is a descendant (or derived)

* Jardine's Naturalists' Library, Vol. X., p. 145.

from the Hatzruden or hounds of the chase, which is, I believe, generally accepted in England, though we do not look upon him as a hound. There is, in my opinion, some danger of the Great Dane becoming too "houndy," and if the Great Dane is considered a hound he is the only representative (although he responds to "pack law") which does not carry his tail erect or like a flag when on the track.

Most people in England who know the breed think that the Great Dane has undeniable claims to be classified as a sporting dog. Dr. Sidney Turner has always taken the greatest interest in this subject, and I cannot do better than quote what he wrote as long ago as 1887*, which is as follows : "I am well aware that Great Danes are now mostly kept for purposes of protection, or perhaps from personal pride ; but I also know that many dogs, such as Fox-terriers, Spaniels, and even Greyhounds, which are classed as sporting, are also kept from similar motives. Two factors are necessary to create sport with dogs—the dog and the game ; the absence of the latter does not prevent a dog being a sporting dog, and the present advanced state of civilisation and consequent effacement of the *feræ naturæ* by reason of the exigencies of cultivation has doubtless prevented many dogs of the larger breeds from exercising the innate but dormant capabilities with which nature has endowed them. Mr. Sanderson, for many years director of the Government Department of Elephants in India, used Mastiffs (of the Bull-Mastiff type) to take leopard, bear, and even small elephant ; but he found it requisite to employ two dogs of greater fleetness to bring the quarry to bay, and allow time for the heavier and more powerful dogs (four) to get up and make the real attack. Now, it seems to me that in Great Danes are combined the requisite qualities—which are so essential to the success of this kind of sport. But it is not to the future possible use, but to the past and recorded evidence of their utility, that I would look for proof of their aptitude and prowess."

Dr. Turner then mentions the old pictures by German, Dutch, and other masters, and especially those of Snyder and Jan Fyt, where dogs similar in type to the modern Great

* "Stock-keeper," April 29, 1887, p. 240.

Dane are depicted in the pursuit of bear and wild boar. Dr. Turner continues : " But it is also a fact that they have been exported to India, Africa, and other parts where large game abound, to be used as sporting dogs. Mr. Adcock says he has seen antelope run down by them in Africa. Now, if it can be shown that they have been, can be, and are used for sporting, why should they not be classed as such ? It is no answer to say many are not so used. One positive is better than a score of negative proofs."

Everything which Dr. Sidney Turner wrote in 1887 applies to-day, only with greater force, as there can be no doubt that Great Danes have been much more used in the last forty years for sporting purposes than was the case previously. It has always been the wish of the Great Dane Club that the breed should be placed in the sporting division, and it is to be hoped that in time the Kennel Club may be able to gratify this wish, as there is really no valid reason for not doing so.

Lastly, I should say that it is quite unknown how the Great Dane came by his name. If Denmark is the country from which these dogs invaded the Continent, the breed has certainly greatly deteriorated in its Fatherland, for the Danish dog of to-day is a very poor specimen compared with the Great Dane.

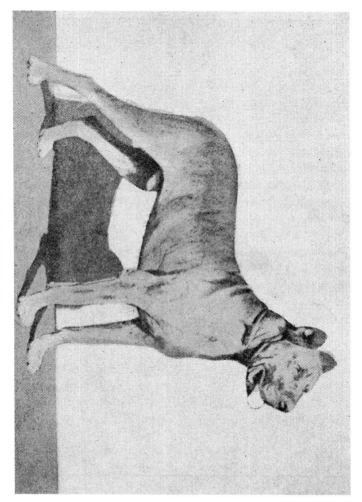

ROLF THE FIRST, 1881.

MEG DODS.

CHAPTER II.

Breeding Principles.

Every breed has certain peculiarities which are usually transmitted from parents to offspring, and the foundation of our breeding principles is based upon a knowledge of these peculiarities (together with the laws of heredity, natural variability, and selection), and consists of modifying families and races in the direction we wish, of increasing their value and usefulness, and improving their appearance by careful selection in mating.

Before proceeding further, it will be as well to briefly consider these laws of heredity, natural variability, and selection to which I have referred.

HEREDITY is the factor by which the characteristics and attributes of parents are transmitted to their offspring. Although we do not know to what extent these various traits are transmitted, there can be no doubt of the fact, or that amongst them are physical characteristics, mental attributes, prolificacy and habits, while natural variations of intellectual characteristics, temperament, and conformation are each transmissible in a greater or lesser degree. The existence of heredity cannot possibly be denied when one knows that definite and distinct breeds could neither be produced or perpetuated unless the offspring resembled the parents to a great extent ; moreover, selection in breeding would be useless but for the fact that the smallest variations may be transmitted, and valuable animals in this way pass on to their offspring their peculiar and desirable characteristics.

If we mate two well-bred Great Danes, we hope that they will have puppies, and if they do we expect them to have the characteristics of Great Danes, and especially the characteristic type of their parents. Heredity thus permits of improvement, and also of natural variation being perpetuated, and it is owing to heredity that two good desirable dogs usually have progeny endowed with their own characteristics.

As an example of this transmission in the concrete, I venture to say that any breeder of experience could tell a dog sired by Boy Bob ex Miss Aileen simply by its characteristics : it was the same with Lord Topper, and Figaro's movement can be traced in the second and third generation. While this tendency of offspring to resemble parents is constant, it becomes stronger in degree the longer any family is bred to a definite standard, and the longer the like ancestry the greater the likelihood of breeding true to type.

There is no doubt that dogs vary greatly in the power which they possess of transmitting their personal characteristics. On the one hand, we find some animals have the power of stamping their attributes on their progeny in the most marked manner, and quite regardless of what those of their mates may be, while on the other hand we find dogs who appear to have no power whatever in this direction. The former class of dogs are said to be prepotent or very powerful in this impressive power.

Natural variations, if they are those we want, are usually found to be very unstable, so that animals who have improved on their parents and are prepotent to a high degree are, or should be, as valuable as they are rare. It is hardly necessary, after what I have said, to mention that by mating animals which both possess some desirable quality, the individual prepotency of the offspring in that quality may be increased, or that the longer this process is continued the greater becomes the probability of the desired attributes being transmitted. What I have said about desirable attributes applies as forcibly, if not more so, to those which are undesirable, as we have in addition to reckon with the power of "throwing back." This "throwing back," though it is probably very much rarer than is generally supposed, undoubtedly exists ; and before going any further, it may be as well to say a few words on this subject, and also deal with "telegony" and

" maternal impressions "—two long-credited beliefs that are almost entirely false, and which, if they have done no serious harm, have at all events done no good to the science of dog breeding.

" Throwing back " is divided by Cossar Ewart into three divisions—Regression, Reversion, and Atavism.

Regression is the phenomenon in which the offspring exhibits more or less mixed up characteristics of its recent and remote ancestors. This may be instanced by the disappearance of a frill or peak in fancy pigeons as sometimes occurs. It is a carrying out of " Galton's law," which states that the two parents between them contribute on the average one half of the inherited faculties, each parent giving one quarter, the four grandparents one quarter or each one-sixteenth, and so on, the sum being $\frac{1}{2} + \frac{1}{4} + \frac{1}{8} + \frac{1}{16}$, etc., $= 1$. Also it is a property that each term of this infinite series is equal to the sum of all those which follow it.

Reversion, according to Ewart, is the phenomenon of the offspring differing more or less from their parents, and exhibiting the characteristics of either some specialised recent ancestor, or of a less specialised common ancestor belonging to the same species. As an example of this, Rabagliati* mentions the appearance of a pure-white calf showing the dark nose and ears and most of the characteristics of our wild white cattle in one of our recognised breeds, he himself having seen it in the Devon Red.

Atavism is the case of an offspring resembling a much more remote ancestor. The occasional appearance of supernumerary digits in the horse is often an example of this.

While I have now given Cossar Ewart's description and division for the benefit of those who would like to draw fine distinctions, I think there is no better definition of " throwing back," in its broad sense, than that of Weissmann, who says :† " By the term is meant the appearance of characteristics which existed in the more remote ancestors, but were absent in the immediate ancestors—i.e., the parents. In other words, there is in each breed, modified by human selection, a pure original type from which the altered breed

* Silvestro Rabagliati, " Veterinary Records," April 3rd, 1904. Et seq.
† " Veterinary Record," May 6th, 1911, p. 709.

has sprung, and we occasionally get characteristics of this original type reproduced generations later in the most perfectly bred animals."

In connection with this subject, it is important to distinguish between phenomena which are due to "throwing back," and those due to arrested development. Dale points out that there has been a good deal of confusion on this point.* He mentions as instances the cases of the nectarine on one hand, and hare lip in the human subject on the other. The nectarine, originally a sport from the peach—in fact, a smooth-skinned peach,—often reverts to the original peach ; at any rate, it so resembles it that it is difficult for even an expert to point out the difference. To suggest, however, that a hare lip in man is a reversion to some ancestral type is a wrong interpretation, the explanation being that it is a case of arrested development due to the fact that at a certain period of fœtal life the nostrils communicate with the outer corners of the mouth.

In summing up, I would say that " throwing back " most certainly occurs, but probably a great deal less frequently than is generally supposed ; and that there is, as De Vries remarks, a sharp line to be drawn between " true reversion " (*i.e.*, " throwing back ") and what he calls " false atavism or vicinism," which is due to crossing. There is no doubt that " crossing " causes the expression of characters which may have lain dormant for generations. It may not be true reversion, as Dale remarks ; it may be that these cases of " false reversion " are really normal Mendelian phenomena ; this, however, is too big a subject to discuss in the present work.†

* " Veterinary Record," May 6th, 1911, p. 709.
† Dr. Osburne writes to me as follows : " With regard to throwing-back, I think it is less rare than you seem to believe ; indeed, I am becoming more and more convinced that it is a common occurrence from numerous instances I have experienced apart from dog breeding. In poultry breeding I often see it. Take that popular breed, Buff Orpington. I have read that before Mr. Cook produced what we look upon now as a typical bird, there were as many as eight different crossings ; he began, I think, with a Black Hamburg and a Buff Cochin—the latter certainly ; and notwithstanding all these crossings in which no other feather-legged bird appeared, one of our greatest and commonest disappointments is to find feathered legs with an otherwise typical specimen—all the remainder of the brood being pure and free. We also find black in the tail feathers, and one or both faults may appear after breeding many chicks absolutely free from both and from the same parents, which are quite pure. Again, we have white appearing in the tail feathers of Black Leghorns in one or two chicks of a brood, when the others are quite free, as are the parents. The Boy Bob and Miss Aileen litters have always had one ' biscuit-fawn ' pup, a remote ancestress whose name I for the moment forget being of this unpleasing colour "

16

CH. VICEROY OF REDGRAVE.

CH. THOR OF REDGRAVE.

The transmission or non-transmission of certain characteristics acquired by mutilation is another controversial
point. I would say at once that characteristics acquired by
mutilation are not transmissible. The cutting of horses,
sheep and dogs' tails has been practised for a very long
while, but it has not produced a single horse, sheep, or dog
that lacks a caudal appendage ; and while from time immemorial the Chinese women have bandaged and crushed
their feet with the view of making them as small as possible,
it has never had the smallest effect on the size of their babies'
feet.*

Finally, I might perhaps mention the transmission of
disease at this point. From an embryological point of view,
there is great doubt as to whether disease can be transmitted,
but there is no doubt whatever that a very strong tendency
or predisposition to disease may be transmitted. Disease
transmission may be divided into those dependent on some
structural alteration and those purely functional to commence
with. The former are much more likely to be influenced by
heredity than the latter.

Telegony (or infection) assumes that a female animal is
tainted by the first male to which she bears offspring, and
some go further and say by subsequent males also. Those
who believe in it think that all subsequent offspring the said
female may bear is liable to show characteristics acquired
from the first or subsequent males which impregnated her ;
or, to put it in the plainest language, that offspring may
resemble a sire which, though not its father, has been previously mated with its dam.

The universal credence given to the theory would incline
one to believe it, but I consider that it is absolutely false.
At the same time, I must mention that Darwin, Spencer, and
Romanes all believed in it, though Darwin changed his mind
before his death. At the present time, I do not think that
there is any man of science who accepts the theory, but a
great many ·farmers, dog breeders and people who have to
do with animals certainly do believe in it. I have discussed

*When Bobtail Sheepdogs and Schipperkes are born tailless, I consider it
the result of selection and heredity. Mr. Theo : Marples writes : " With
regard to Bobtail Sheepdogs and Schipperkes, in both cases I find on inquiry
that the majority of puppies are born with full tails, some with stumps, and
a very small percentage tailless."

D

the matter with many of them, and though the majority of them believed it, they were not able to produce a single actual example, or even one that had come within their personal experience. All the cases reported, even those which at first sight appear most convincing, are open to grave doubt. What is quite as important is that there exists abundant evidence to the contrary. To mention only one case : Professor Cossar Ewart, being anxious to prove the existence of telegony, mated a male zebra, a particularly prepotent animal, with a number of mares of different breed and type, about twenty hybrids resulting. The following season the mares were mated with stallions of their own species, the progeny in no instance showing any indication that the dam had previously been mated with a zebra. In a summary on a discussion of the subject, Professor Thomson says : " Experiments proved this at least, that telegony does not generally occur, even when what were considered to be favourable conditions were secured ; indeed, anything suggestive of telegony occurred only in a very small percentage of cases. Moreover, when peculiar phenomena of inheritance were observed, they seemed to be readily explicable on the reversion hypothesis."*

MATERNAL IMPRESSION.—The belief in the theory of maternal impression is quite as widely spread as that of telegony, and equally fails on close examination. It is one of the oldest superstitions, dating back to the time of Jacob.† It extends to all classes, and is applied not only to domesticated animals, but to the human race as well. There is no doubt that a violent shock to a human mother may produce the most serious results, may arrest the development of the foetus, or even provoke miscarriage ; and it is quite a common thing to find birthmarks, malformations, hairiness, peculiarities of colour, and any or every physical abnormality attributed to some shock or impression sustained by the mother during pregnancy. People think that because a shock can produce miscarriage anything else abnormal about the child is

* Dr. Osburne writes : " I agree with you that this (infection) does not occur, though generally believed in by farmers and others, even well-educated persons. Not only so, but a friend of mine, who farms, told me of a belief still more incredible, and what he himself heard stated at a lecture on agricultural matters, given by a paid lecturer—viz., that if a bull is mated to a cow possessing some peculiar characteristics, he becomes so infected by her that, when he is next mated to a second cow, she may, and often does, produce a calf showing the same peculiarities as the former cow."
† Genesis, Chap. XXX., Verse 37.

18

also due to some shock, one coincidence being taken as proof of the fact while a million on the other side are overlooked. The belief is held most strongly in the North of England and Scotland, and all manner of plans are carried out to obtain some desired end. For instance, if a red calf is wanted, the cow is blindfolded before being mated, and when the covering is taken from her eyes the first object to meet her outlook is a red heifer. Many similar examples might be cited. To show what great credence the belief has obtained, Rabagliati* mentions an experienced dog breeder who told him that if a Bull-terrier were mated with a dog of the same breed in absolute darkness, and when there was sufficient light to see, that the bitch found herself amongst Greyhounds, and was kept with them (all possibility of connection being prevented) for some time, her litter would present absolutely unmistakable characteristics of the Greyhound. This is of course absurd. As the same author remarks, one might as well expect if the Bull-terrier had been kept amongst cows, that it would develop characteristics of a bovine nature.

SATURATION.†—The theory of saturation is more recent than those I have just discussed ; but it is quite as strongly believed in by its advocates. As far as I can understand, they believe that the body of the mother as a result of conception, takes on certain characteristics of the male parent ; that through the fœtus the mother becomes saturated with the blood and nature of the male parent, and that this change is systemic. Some people even say that changes take place in the mother herself, and that as years go by she approximates more and more in appearance to the male unit. It is common knowledge that married couples happily united grow more and more alike one another ; but is it due to saturation ? May not the cause of the change be environment ? Persons of the same type and appearance very frequently have the same tastes and mode of life. May not the converse be true ? In my opinion, it is quite as likely, and I am not aware of any evidence of value that will bear scrutiny and support the theory of saturation.

Having now dealt with the subjects of throwing back,

* Veterinary Records, April 3rd, 1904, et seq.
† Thomas H. Dale, M.R.C.V.S., Gov. Vet. Surgeon, Potchefstroom, The Veterinary Record," April 29th, 1911.

telegony, maternal impression, and saturation, all of which are so connected with heredity as to require mention, we can return to the subject we were discussing.

NATURAL VARIABILITY.—Every animal varies to a greater or lesser degree from its parents and its litter mates. These differences may be due to a "throwing back" or to a combination of old traits giving the appearance of a fresh peculiarity ; but, quite apart from these, it is sure that there is a tendency to vary to a certain extent, and that this tendency, like other attributes, is transmitted and is so constant that no two living things are exactly similar.

It is this variability which enables the breeder to improve the breed, while the law that every animal differs to a certain extent from parents and offspring ensures him material for selection. Lastly, the law of inheritance enables him to perpetuate desirable variations by proper mating and judicious surroundings.

SELECTION.—If the principle of inheritance were fixed, and the offspring inherited the attributes of their parents, and those alone, improvement would be impossible ; but, thanks to the law of natural variability, some of the offspring are better than their parents, and so we get progressive improvement. As I mentioned in connection with prepotency, the progression may be in the direction of amelioration or deterioration, and the latter can only be avoided by improving the desirable variations by proper mating and suitable surroundings.

Inbreeding is the mating of animals more or less closely related, in which case the characteristics of the parents are intensified and strengthened in the offspring by the two similar hereditary forces. By inbreeding, the blood of superior animals is concentrated, and the more it is concentrated the greater will be the resemblance of the offspring to one another and to their parents, and the greater will be the probability of improved characteristics becoming fixed, and so hereditary or transmissible from parent to offspring.

The chief value of an inbred dog lies in its power of impressing its qualities or characteristics on its offspring, and the longer and closer the blood relationship the greater will be the resemblance between parent and offspring. The

Photo., Hedges.

CH. TIGER OF CLEETHORPES.

CH. VRELST OF REDGRAVE.

evil results of inbreeding are a deterioration in size, bone, prolificacy, and mental vigour, while any slight physical failing may so develop that it becomes a deformity and a slight constitutional weakness may be increased until it grows seriously dangerous. It will thus be seen that inbreeding cannot be lightly practised, and only by following Nature's law of selecting the fittest and rejecting all others can inbreeding be tried with the view of increasing desired characteristics in comparative safety. As a matter of fact, I would never advise any beginner to attempt the practice, and those of more mature experience will be wise if they never employ it except when they wish to permanently fix in a family some particular characteristic which occurs by natural variation in only one or two of them, or else when they want to rapidly secure a desirable uniformity of good points.*

* Dr. Osburne writes : " I do not know how far I am in agreement with you as regards the vexed question of inbreeding ; it is very possible we hold the same, or nearly the same, views. For myself, I hold a very strong belief, come to after considerable study and consideration of various theories and close observation. My belief is that so long as parents are sound, free from any weakness or defect, and are of correct or the desirable type, inbreeding may be practised to almost any extent. Inbreeding in itself will not result in deterioration in size, bone, mental vigour, or prolificacy, so long as these are not found in, or handed down by, the parents. On the other hand, my belief is equally strong that it is not only desirable, but almost essential to success, to breed from sound, healthy, and typical parents that are closely related, whether it be in the animal or the vegetable kingdom. A large number of persons would throw up their hands in horror were they to be told this, but I think it is only because they have not thought the matter out for themselves, and have accepted a theory that has been handed down for generations, until it has become almost a superstition that a " change of blood " is necessary to keep a stock healthy. How often does one hear in the case of a person suffering from some mental affection or defect, or who is born with some physical deformity : ' Well, what could you expect from a marriage of first cousins ? ' " forgetting the 101 causes to which the affliction may be due. I will assert without fear of contradiction that in such cases I have very seldom missed finding in the family history quite sufficient to account for all the trouble, though infinite pains is frequently taken to hide it. On the other hand, look at the number of unions of near relatives that are not followed by any disastrous results. No one will attempt to deny that where a family taint or some defect or weakness is present, it may not only be handed down to the offspring, but will almost certainly be enhanced and aggravated by such a marriage of relatives. When two good specimens are mated, and the mating turns out satisfactorily, resulting in typical pups, then I would not hesitate to inbreed in order to fix the type."

The above is Dr. Osburne's opinion, and, coming from a man of such knowledge and experience, both with human beings and dogs, is entitled to the greatest respect and consideration. I am sorry to say that I cannot agree with him altogether—that is, if I rightly understand what he has written. A great deal depends on what is meant by inbreeding. It is quite true that if we consider our best dogs, the majority have one or two common ancestors, especially in the third or fourth generations ; and this, I think, there is no objection to when a good outcross is occasionally introduced. It is when we come to nearer and more recent relations that one has to be careful : the mating of cousins should be very carefully considered ; and, however perfect the dogs may be, I am absolutely sure, in my own mind, that repeated interbreeding of cousins will result in deterioration and sterility. It is all right for a fancier of Dr. Osburne's experience to arrange his matings so that the same animals appear three or four times in the third and fourth generations, and even to mate cousins ; but it is a very different thing for a beginner or a fancier of even two or three years to attempt doing such things.

Mr. Jefferies, who inbred to a considerable extent in making his "Stone" strain of Bulldogs and has a large experience, believes that it does not matter really how much you inbreed on the father's side but that you must not press it on the mother's side.

Every dog has a pedigree, for it simply means ancestry, and may be known or not ; but, from the practical breeder's point of view, it means the fixation of a certain type or certain characteristics. Pedigree, therefore, is useful as a means of ascertaining whether the family of a dog has been bred to one standard type. If so, the longer the pedigree the better, and the value of the animal with the pedigree lies in its power of impressing its family characteristics, while the pedigree itself is valuable according as this power has been fixed in the family, and according as the near ancestors rather than the more remote are pre-eminently good, for it is the blood of the immediate ancestors which predominates ; the uniformity of type and individual excellence of the near ancestors being much more important than the mere length of pedigree.

Much has been written about the relative influence of male and female parent in respect to the offspring ; but, out of all the different theories that have been propounded, only one has received much attention. This theory is that the male is especially prepotent in transmitting conformation, while the female transmits the inward characteristics. It is probably dependent on the fact that there is a great external likeness to the male parent among young domestic animals, which is, in my opinion, the result of the much greater care that is usually taken in choosing the male parent. The comparative neglect in selecting bitches which I cannot help thinking is very extensive in England, is one of the greatest errors which is made. I think it quite as important that the bitch should be as good a one as the dog, for, besides her original half share in the puppy, she has to nourish it from her own substance, and subsequently, when it is born, she has to instruct it.

In selecting the parents, we should as a starting point choose those dogs which most closely resemble our ideal ; they should be dogs which show the greatest possible number of desirable qualities, with the ability to stamp these qualities on their offspring, while at the same time having the greatest freedom from objectionable points. Although a good family history is important, it must be remembered that it is equally important to have a good individual as parent. It is absurd to think that all the members of a superior race will be uniformly superior, or that parents are sure to transmit esteemed characters which they do not themselves possess, though perhaps their immediate relations do ; and it must not be forgotten that defects are more readily transmitted than are valued qualities.

The importance of the parents resembling each other in their good points lies in the fact that the closer these points are matched, the greater will be the probability of their being perpetuated and intensified in the offspring.

As Mr. R. E. Nicholas has pointed out, the value of selection lies in its positive or cumulative tendency. It is slow, but it is sure, permanent and free from risks.

SELECTION OF BITCH.—In choosing the bitch, it is best for the beginner, if he can afford it, to buy a bitch that has been bred from once or twice before. She should be the best that he can afford, absolutely healthy, and physically as perfect as possible, while she should belong to a family where excellence is the rule and inferiority the exception. She must come of a good breeding stock—that is to say, of a strain noted for its fecundity and its well-developed maternal instincts—and it is important that she should possess all the good points to which her pedigree owes its excellence. Finally, having satisfied himself as to the pedigree, it will be as well for the breeder to see as many of her near relations as possible, and make certain that they are typical animals and uniform, for the family in which no two members resemble each other should be carefully avoided.

SELECTION OF SIRE.—The same lines should be followed in selecting the sire as the dam, and he should be sound, healthy, of great vigour and essentially masculine. As I have already pointed out, there is a most lamentable custom in England to only consider the sire, and few people have profited by the example of Mrs. Horsfall, who built up her wonderful kennel as much by the excellence of her bitches as of her dogs. The beginner, as a rule, though he does not trouble himself about the dam, insists on having a big prize-winner as the sire and there is, of course, some sense in his decision, as the best stud dogs are generally members of a family which has been successful on the benches. There are, however, objections to this plan, as the life of a show dog is seldom conducive to good breeding qualities, while many successful animals are used so often as to seriously detract from their value as sires.

In conclusion, it may be said that the animals mated should be chosen because they are representative of the type of their family. It is important to study the offspring of different good sires, even if they belong to the same family, as they frequently vary in impressive power to such an extent that one or two, though of great personal excellence, reproduce their desirable qualities very poorly and with such great irregularity that they may be worse than useless as sires.

The more the parents resemble one another in their good qualities, the more probable it is that good qualities will be inherited, and the greater will probably be the likeness between the parents and their offspring ; family excellence, however, is of more importance than any individual good points, and this is an important point to remember. For instance, supposing we have an otherwise excellent bitch with a long back, we ought not to mate her with a dog who has an excessively short back, as if we do the puppies will be a mixture of too long and too short backs. The proper course to pursue is to find a dog from a family where the backs have been of the right length for as many generations as possible, and mate him with your long-backed bitch. It cannot be too strongly insisted that it is an absolute delusion to imagine that two opposite characters in the parents balance one another in the offspring ; in other words, the compensative theory of breeding is absolutely fallacious, and will only lead to disappointment in the end.

After we have bred one litter and have reared those we originally selected, it is of great importance, of course, that we should improve our stock, which can only be done by selection on the lines we used in choosing our sire and dam. It is often hard to do so, especially with puppies we have reared and perhaps spent a great deal of time and trouble over, but we must get rid of all our dogs that are below the average type and dogs that are infertile or do not transmit their family characters ; other animals which we must dispose of are those which show any signs of constitutional weakness, bad doers, shy breeders, and any that are miscoloured, unless of such wonderful excellence as to justify their being kept.

As regards the age at which to breed from a Great Dane, a bitch should never be bred from at her first season. This usually occurs at the age from seven to ten months, and is therefore the very time at which the most active and important growth is proceeding in our breed. As an immense amount of vitality is given up by the bitch to her offspring, it follows that her growth is bound to be arrested, and her stamina deteriorated if we allow her to have puppies at the very time when all the food she takes should be used in building up her frame. While it is inadvisable to breed from bitches at the first season, it is, I consider, most important that they should be bred from at the next opportunity. At the second œstrum, which occurs any time after the bitch is a year old, the bones of the pelvis (hips) are not completely ossified or fixed ; consequently there is some mobility or pliancy. If the bitch happens to be a small one, and the puppy to be born large, this is of the greatest value, as it allows the ring of bone through which the puppy passes at its birth to expand. If breeding is put off till after the second œstrum, the bones are a rigid ring, there is no yielding, and many a bitch has lost her life on this account. The age at which a dog should be used is about the same as the bitch—viz., on an average, about fifteen months, or when they are nearly full grown. The sexual instinct is, of course, developed early in all animals, and for this reason young dogs should be carefully separated from any bitch in season. Personally, I believe in separating the dogs from the bitches when about three months old, and there can be no doubt that young dogs left in proximity to bitches in season suffer for it, and are occasionally affected by it for the remainder of their lives, being unreliable as stockgetters, and savage.

It is a great mistake to breed from a bitch too often ; once a year is quite sufficient, though twice in succession with a strong bitch of three years may do no harm. Still, the breeder who is wise will only breed at alternate seasons, and will be repaid by better puppies and the undamaged constitution of the bitch.

25

The best time of year for puppies to be born is probably the end of January or in February, as they will then have the natural heat of their dam to keep them warm for six weeks, and have the spring and summer, when it is naturally warm, in which to make their early growth. I think there can be no doubt that, as a rule, puppies born at this time are stronger and less liable to illness, and some experienced fanciers are so firmly of this opinion that they absolutely refuse to breed during the summer.

In the advertisements of certain stud dogs, I frequently notice that the owner draws attention to the extraordinary number of puppies his dog has sired in its last litter.* A very prolific stockgetter is of no advantage ; it is, in fact, the reverse. This should be especially remembered by the beginner and a certain type of fancier who only wants to make money, for, besides not being remunerative, I think it has done a great deal of harm to the genuine Dane lover. The sooner people realise that it is the quality, and not the quantity, of puppies in a litter which is of importance, the better it will be for the Great Dane fancy. It should be a cardinal rule that every mismarked, weak, or weedy puppy should be instantly destroyed. Instead of this, as I have said, many people get foster mothers and rear every specimen, even the weakest and worst, quite regardless of the fact that they are doing infinite damage to their own reputation as Great Dane breeders, and to that of their dogs as sires.

To briefly sum up, the would-be breeder should carefully consider his ideal of the Great Dane. Having made up his mind, he should compare his standard with the ideal type as formulated by the Great Dane Club under the advice of the leading breeders and judges, and also see if it agrees with the type of the most prominent winning dogs. If he finds his ideal is not in accordance with the accepted type, that it

---

* " It seems to me that this class of advertisement is framed and is also generally read upon wrong premises. The number of puppies depends upon the number of egg-cells (ova) developed in the ovary of the bitch, discharged into the womb at the periodic time of ' heat,' and there fertilised by the male-cells (spermatozoa) of the dog. Now the spermatic fluid of any normal, fertile dog that is not weakened by age, improper feeding, or excessive service contains abundant male-cells to fertilise all the healthy and mature egg-cells present in the womb of the bitch at the time of mating. In the absence of these egg-cells, which are only produced by the female, there can be no off-spring, no matter how vigorous the male. Viewed from this standpoint, the size of the litter is seen to depend upon the bitch rather than the dog, provided the latter be ordinarily fertile and vigorous."—R. E. Nicholas.

26

approaches more to the Greyhound or the Mastiff, he will be wise not to attempt to breed. The Great Dane is a breed quite apart from the Mastiff or the Greyhound, not a cross, as some people seem to imagine ; and any attempt to breed away from the accepted type will only end in bitter disappointment, both on the bench and at stud. The object of every breeder should be to produce dogs which, besides satisfying him, will be successful on the bench. If he can do this he will find that the pecuniary side of the matter will take care of itself, though this should not be allowed to influence one in breeding. The person who only or chiefly thinks of what he will make had better give up Great Danes. The true Dane lover will be more than satisfied with the knowledge that he has bred a first-class specimen, and the beginner who follows the advice given in this chapter will be far more likely to do so than the older fancier who trusts to his own intuition and the " light of nature."

CHAPTER III.

—

The Main Breeding Points.

It is a difficult thing to say what are the most important
points to breed for in a Great Dane, as the ideal dog has so
many noticeable physical characteristics, a failure in any
one often seriously affecting the " general appearance " which
is so all-important.

Personally, I consider size, type, soundness, spirit and colour
are the most essential points ; and if our dogs are pre-eminent
in these, they may fail slightly in others, but will still be in
the first rank.

To take the five points in their order : it is a question of
opinion as to what is a " tall " Great Dane. According to
the Great Dane Club standard, the minimum height is 30in.
for a dog and 28in. for a bitch. I should like to see this
increased to 31in. and 29in., as I do not consider nearly
enough importance is paid to size. Other things being
equal, the difference in value between a 33 and a 34in. Dane
is out of all proportion to the 1in. difference of height.

In the original numerical standard of points drawn up
by the Great Dane Club, no marks were given for a 30in.
dog, 2 for a 31in. dog, 4 for a 32in., 6 for a 33in., 9 for a 34in.,
and 13 for a 35in. dog ; the proportionate marks being the
same for the inches in a bitch from 28 to 33in.

Personally, I believe that 35in. is about as large as we most
of us see, though I would not say that 36in. is impossible.

At the great Ranelagh Show in 1885, which I well remember,
Mr. Rawdon Lee measured several dogs, the two tallest
being Mr. Reginald Herbert's Leal (33¾in.) and Mr. Riego's

Photo., C. Bellinger.

CH. BOY BOB.

Photo., C. Bellinger.

CH. PRIMLEY PRODIGAL.

Cid Campeador (33½in.), while Cedric the Saxon measured 33¼in.

Mr. Rawdon Lee makes mention in his book of Sir Roger Palmer's Sam, saying that he was 35in.,* and that he had never seen a Great Dane approaching him in size ; but the suggestion that it was quite exceptional is certainly wrong, as both Mr. Boyes' Chance of Rosedale and Mr. A. T. Walker's Monarch of Ansdell were 35in., while Herr Esser describes Otho of Waveney as 36in.† I have myself measured Otho, and seen him measured, but never made him more than 34½in., which only shows how differently people will measure, for though of course a dog varies considerably in height from one time to another, I do not think it would ever amount to 1½in.

Of Great Danes in the early part of last century, Lord Mount Edgcombe has a painting of one said to be 36in. at the shoulder, and has in addition the skeleton of the dog, which corroborates the statement. The Marquis of Hastings had also a picture of a buff-and-white Great Dane measuring 36in., which was painted by Clifford de Tomsan in 1803 (Vero Shaw).

There seems little doubt that the great American dog, Mr. Butler's Prince, was 36in., while as the climax Vero Shaw mentions a Boarhound at Cologne of 37in., "measured by a person accustomed to the breed." He evidently does not believe it, however, as he entirely agrees with Herr Lang, who writes that "formerly these dogs were not larger than they are to-day, the assumed height of 36in. only being given in untrustworthy pictures."

I might add that Sydenham Edwards (1803) says "he (the Great Dane) was usually about 28in., occasionally 31in." ; that Richardson speaks of the dog as "gigantic," 30 to 31in. ; while Buffon gives the height as 28in.

In concluding the subject of height, it should be stated that on the Continent an inch or two less in height is not considered to handicap a black, blue or harlequin ; but

* Vero Shaw in his "Book of the Dog," p. 505, says he was 34in.
† "Our Dogs," July, 1908, p. 467.

I am glad to say they are all judged by the same standard in this country.*

There is in my mind very little doubt that a tendency to size is inherited as well as other form characteristics ; but it must be remembered that size more than anything else depends on the postnatal treatment of the puppies. No matter how tall or of what colour a Dane may be, he must above everything else be true to *type*. We frequently see those huge unwieldy creatures, often the tallest dogs in the show, and whose colour is not always objectionable, but which, except in breeding and name, are an insult to this graceful and dignified breed. The coarse skull, head and neck, thick tail, clumsy round bone, and bulky outline are features that are too often handed down to succeeding generations, and are characteristics which cannot be considered as conforming with the type of the Dane, which above all must be graceful and endowed with an activity which is free from clumsiness, a feature impossible in the coarse animals described above.

Soundness is most important, and though it is largely dependent on the rearing and exercising of the puppies, it is distinctly a point to breed for. The initial soundness in the new-born puppies which is so desirable can only be obtained by uniting two absolutely healthy parents, dogs who show this characteristic, and whose family history presents an absolutely clean record and a freedom from any undesirable traits. I have already pointed out that faults are more easily transmitted than good points, and every breeder of experience has seen some slight failing reproduced in successive generations which can often be traced to one particular dog.

Spirit is essential in a Great Dane, as without it he cannot have that general appearance, " Vim," or " Go "—call it what you will,—which should characterise the breed. He should look and hold himself as if he were Lord of the Universe, and as if all other animals existed only on sufferance and by his permission. He has the strength of a young lion, with the vivacity of a terrier ; and though he should be trained to

* Since writing the above, Mr. W. R. Temple informs me that he saw a harlequin Great Dane at the White City, belonging to Mr. Hagenbeck, in 1909, which after measuring several times he made a good 36in. Mr. Temple measures in a way that I have never seen previously used, and there can be no doubt as to the correctness of his measurements.

keep his exuberant spirit in subjection, he should still possess it. This, of course, like soundness, can only be obtained by careful selection and proper feeding of the breeding stock.

I am one of those who think that the Great Dane has now arrived at such a pitch of excellence in England that the colour question is all-important, and that we cannot be too careful in trying to produce clean colours. Of course, if it is a question between colour and type, we must have type as long as the colour is not impossible ; but it should not be too much to ask fanciers to pay every consideration to colour nowadays, seeing the excellence of the dogs which we have to choose from in each colour. I have the greatest sympathy for those who hold an opposite opinion (though I am glad to say they are in the small minority), for there is nothing more disappointing than to have an almost perfect dog which is miscoloured. I think it is much the best plan to destroy all miscoloured puppies at once, as it saves great disappointment, but if they are kept for some reason or other, and prove to be dogs of splendid type, they should only be used to breed from in the hope that a clean-coloured dog may result ; they should never be shown. It is all very well to say that a good dog, like a good horse, may be of any colour. I must also quote the saying that "a good horse cannot be a bad colour," neither can a good Dane be a bad colour, for if the colour is bad he cannot be considered a good Dane. It does not hold good with other breeds ; why should it with Great Danes ? The Great Dane, moreover, is greatly dependent on his general appearance, so that colour must enter into the question. If we were to see the most beautiful woman in a delightfully designed gown made of the most lovely materials, but the colours of the dress were crude and incongruous, she would certainly take second place as a " picture " to a slightly less beautiful woman perfectly dressed in colours that were in harmony ; and I think the same holds good with dogs—or Great Danes, at any rate.

The recognised colours at the present time are Black, Blue, and Fawn ("whole colours"), Brindles and Harlequins, and they will be more minutely mentioned in the Standard of Points (Chapter VI.). When the Great Dane Club was formed in 1882, the colours in the Club book were described as the "various shades of grey (commonly termed blue), red, black, or pure white, or white with patches of the above-mentioned colours." "The above ground colours," the Club's standard goes on to say, "appear in the brindles, and are also the ground colour of the mottled specimens. The mottled specimens have irregular patches or clouds upon the above-named ground colours ; in some cases the clouds or markings being of two or more tints." It will thus be seen that in the early days there was a much greater latitude, and though the colour question was always present, it was very different from what it is to-day.

As regards breeding for colour, to obtain good fawns and brindles we should mate a fawn with a brindle. By following this plan it will be found that in the case of brindles a much better ground colour will be obtained with darker and more sharply defined stripes. If brindles are mated together the colour degenerates until it is almost black, while if fawns are united the colour gradually becomes a muddy yellow.

I might here mention that while the ground colour of brindles may be from the lightest yellow to the darkest, it is the light-golden brindle that is especially appreciated in Germany. I cannot say that I have noticed that English judges have any special predilection in this matter.

Blacks should be bred from blacks or from black-and-white harlequins, while blues and blacks also produce a good black. In Germany they do not consider a black bred from a brindle is a pure black, only those bred from harlequin stock are considered pure.

Blues are properly bred from blues or blues and blacks.

Harlequins should be obtained from harlequins, or from harlequins and blacks (the latter probably give the best results), and there is no reason at the present time for breeding them otherwise. Ten years ago there were so few good harlequin sires that people took the risk of mating a harlequin with a good brindle sire on the off-chance of there being one or two harlequins. This, of course, is absolutely wrong in principle, and was seldom successful, though in one instance it actually happened that two harlequin champions were born in a litter by a brindle from a harlequin. It was

32

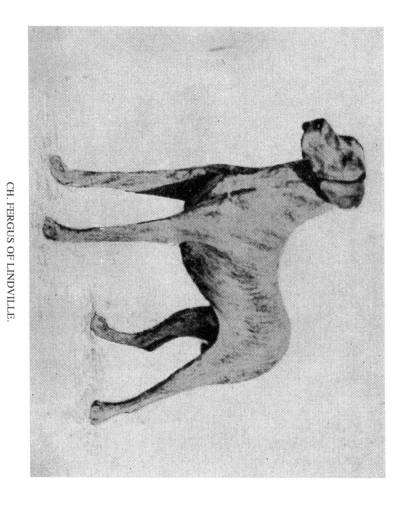

CH. FERGUS OF LINDVILLE.

VICEREGENT OF REDGRAVE.

deplorable that both died in their early prime, but at the same time they could never have been depended upon to breed harrequins, and the importation of Brutus von Lichtenrade (Figaro of St. Austell), Ch. Tilly Salgau, and Greenhill Squire has now placed the harlequins in such a position that they have lately been more successful than any other colour, and there can be no possible reason for mating opposed colours in future.

The mode in which the white first appeared in the harlequin has been much discussed, as the original Great Dane was probably a blue. It has been suggested that the white came from a cross with the St. Bernard, which was undoubtedly crossed with the Great Dane by the monks of the Hospice in 1815, when they found their own breed greatly degenerating. This would seem an adequate explanation but for the fact that we have pictures of black-and-white Great Danes painted much earlier than this date. I can only say that I have never found any explanation which is entirely satisfactory.

In considering old paintings and works on the breed, it makes the belief possible that in reality the harlequins and blacks are a distinct breed of dogs, as also are the brindles and fawns, and possibly the blues. The idea that these are distinct breeds rather than families is strengthened by a study of their anatomical features and temperaments. Surely there is more difference between the harlequin Dane and the fawn than there is between the Irish and English Setters. Also, I understand that the different coloured Danes are judged by different standards on the Continent. I do not for a moment wish to support the view that the different colours are different breeds, but I think it right to mention a view which is at all events held by some Great Dane fanciers.

Besides the five what I may call cardinal points, there are many other important ones to be bred for, and it is only right to say that one should aim at them all. Some, however, are more important than others, and this is what I wish to make clear in this chapter.

33

CHAPTER IV.

Desirable Points and Defects.

Undesirable points or defects are, as must be obvious to anyone, any characteristics that are at variance with the generally accepted standard of the Great Dane. Before starting to describe them, it might be well to give the list of the most important defects as published by the Great Dane Club in 1882, and then compare them with those of the present day as we proceed. The list of defects published was :—" Too heavy a head, too highly arched a frontal bone and deep stop or indentation between the eyes ; large ears and hanging flat to face, short neck, full dewlap ; too narrow or too broad a chest ; sunken or hollow or quite straight back ; bent forelegs, over-bent fetlocks ; twisted feet ; spreading toes ; too heavy and much bent or too highly carried tail, or with brush underneath ; weak hindquarters and a general want of muscle."

Of the various characteristics in this list, all of which are of course faults, I consider that those which relate to the limbs are the most important, as they signify a want of soundness which we have given as one of the cardinal points. Of course, a great deal depends on what we call unsoundness, and many youngsters show a slight bend in the legs, out of which they will grow, or which can be rectified by exercise ; but a full-grown dog with bent legs or weak hindquarters, or one that goes down on his hocks, is certainly not sound, and not fit to win a first prize. One of the chief characteristics of a Great Dane is his wonderful activity and movement, and he cannot have these if his legs are crooked or give way. We naturally breed for straight legs by choosing perfectly sound parents, as bad legs may possibly be inherited through a rickety or family idiosyncrasy; they may, however, also be acquired through sprains, poor feeding, or faulty exercise. With the latter three causes I shall deal in the rearing of puppies, as they can be greatly remedied; if the crookedness is due to rickets, I do not believe there is any true remedy, and the best thing will be to destroy the animal, though it can almost always be prevented by proper nourishment of the dam and puppies if treated sufficiently early.

For a long while—in fact, until quite recently—a good head seemed the "be all and the end all" of a Great Dane's qualifications; and if the dog only possessed a good, long, narrow head, many judges seemed quite oblivious to the importance of body, legs, neck, or anything else. Dr. Sidney Turner has pointed out that "the head is a sort of fifth limb, and if the shafts of the long bones are of unusual length, the bones of the cranium naturally follow the same law, and *vice versa.*" It used to be considered that the longer and leaner a Dane's head, the better it was; but this is not the case. A head which measured 13½in. from occipital protuberance to tip of nose would be quite out of place in a dog measuring 31in. at the shoulder, as it would be out of all proportion as regards length, being much too long; and *a Great Dane must, before everything, be symmetrical or properly balanced.* Nor are size and power in the head necessarily synonymous with coarseness, as some people seem to think. The cheeks should not be perfectly flat, as until recently it has been the custom to describe them; but should show development, which point, I am glad to say, is at last beginning to be appreciated. Absolute flatness would denote non-development of the *masseter* or cheek muscle, and would signify an absence of power, while also depriving the head of character. Herr Gustav Lang writes that "a dog with flat cheeks has lost the character of a Dogge" (*i.e.,* a Great Dane), and I entirely agree with him.

35

The muzzle or foreface is proportionately broad, and the skull proper is proportionately narrow, so that when looked at from in front and above the whole head appears to be much the same breadth.

The nostrils should be large, wide and open; there should be a slight ridge where the bone joins the cartilage,* and the end of the nose should be distinctly blunt.

The muzzle or foreface may be at fault in two or three respects, when it is known as " snipey," " snouty " or " lippy," though the first adjective is frequently made to include two distinct faults. In the snipey muzzle proper the foreface narrows too rapidly, and comes to somewhat of a point ; this gives the face a somewhat mean expression, even though the depth of the muzzle is almost the same from before back, as it should be. In the snouty muzzle proper there is a deficiency of bone in the lower jaw towards the anterior end, so that instead of the upper and lower lines of the muzzle being parallel, or nearly so, they diverge more and more as they approach the skull. Occasionally we get a combination of the snipey with the snouty nose, and this of course is worse than either alone. I have heard it discussed and, I think, seen it questioned in print, as to whether a snouty nose can be artificially rectified. For the casual observer it most certainly can be made to appear cured, as continual massage and drawing down the lip will so lengthen it that its lower line hides the deficiency of bone ; an experienced judge, however, would not be imposed upon by this trick, or at all events ought not to be so. This is the condition known as lippiness, and it is possible that at times it may be natural.

The lower line of the muzzle should be parallel with the top line of the nose bones when the head is viewed in profile. If it is not parallel, it is either because there is deficiency of bone as above - mentioned or because there is a super-abundance of skin under the throat (dewlap). This last occurs when the skin of the skull is not tight enough to draw up the skin under the jaw and the skin of the neck, and so make the lines parallel. Dewlap is especially common in blue Danes, and this fact has led certain Continental fanciers

* As a matter of fact, having boiled down several skulls, Mr. Cornish-Bowden informs me that this ridge occurs on the bone above the junction of bone and cartilage, that is to say nearer the eye and not at the junction.

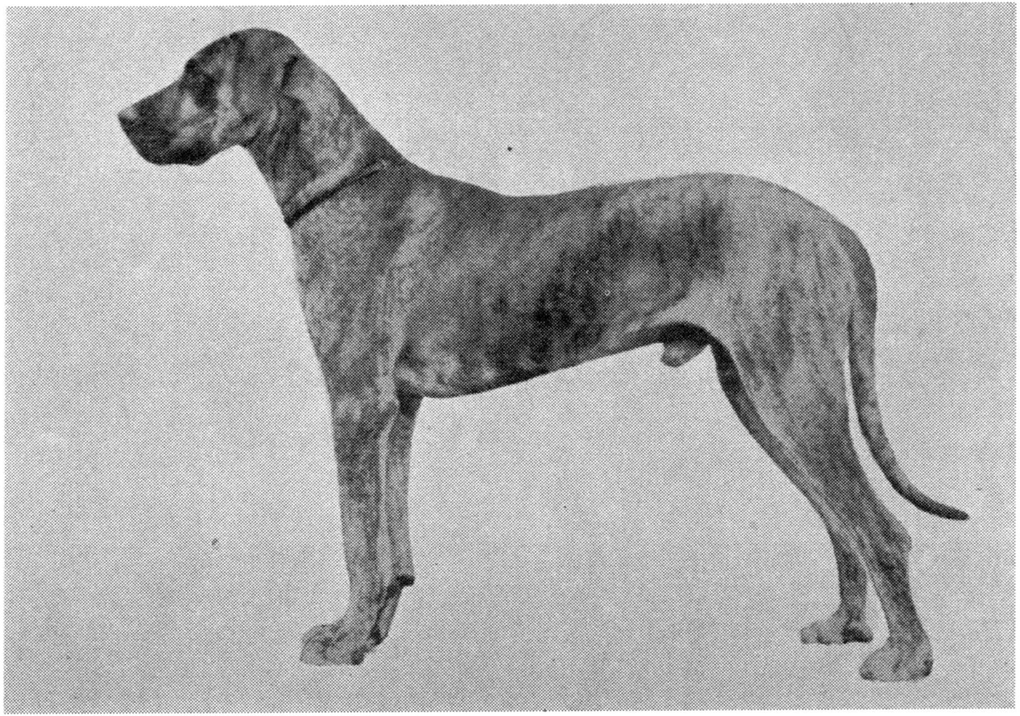

GRANT OF AXWELL.

CH. VIOLA OF REDGRAVE.

to conclude that the skin of a blue is of a different consistency—more elastic, I imagine they would say—than that of other colours. The appearance of a want of parallelism between the upper and lower lines of the muzzle is also seen if the stop (or rise at the forehead) is not sufficient or is too marked. The former gives the face a coarse and somewhat stupid expression, while the latter makes a head too much resembling a Pointer's.

I think that the majority of our best dogs are inclined, if anything, to have too little stop. If we compare them with the best German dogs, ours are certainly deficient in stop, and a want of it, in my opinion, certainly detracts from the appearance of great intelligence which the dog should possess.

The eyes should be as dark as possible, round and small, expressive and alert, not set too close, and with well-developed eyebrows, which contribute as much as anything to a sharp and expectant expression. Harlequins are allowed eyes of any colour, and eyes of a lighter shade than in the blacks, brindles and fawns are allowed in blues, but the darker they are the better.

The points I have so far mentioned in connection with head are points that we can only influence by a most careful selection of the parents ; but the next point (the ears) and the neck are not only influenced by the parents, but by the treatment the puppies receive after they are born.

The ears are, perhaps, of all the adjuncts of the head, the most important so far as the actual expression of the dog is concerned ; and if they are faulty, much can be done to remedy what is wrong. They should, as the Great Dane Club standard says, be "small, set high on the skull, and carried slightly erect, with the tips falling forward." The smaller they are the better, and it is most important that they should be set on high, as, if well carried, it gives a far more alert expression. Those dogs who have their ears set on low almost invariably have a sleepy expression, and I do not think that I have ever seen one that carried its ears—which are generally large—in a proper way. At the same time, even if a dog has small ears and they are set on properly, he does not always carry them well, and this may be due to several causes. In the first place, a young puppy does not carry his ears up ; they are always or almost always down, and it is only after a month or two that he begins to carry them properly. The puppy may be greatly assisted to get his ears up by having him with you and constantly attracting his attention, as each time he is called he will turn round and prick up his ears, and this will gradually get him into the habit of keeping them up. Another cause of ears hanging badly is the consistency of the cartilage in them. The cartilage exists, of course, in all dogs' ears ; but in some it is so thin as to be almost inappreciable, and in these the ears can only be made to hang properly with the greatest difficulty, if at all. I have known dogs the cartilage of whose ears was so deficient that they could not even have been cropped properly. Something can be done to benefit the faulty hang of these ears, but I am doubtful as to the remedy being very successful, though it certainly is in the third class of cases, which are those in which the fold in the ear is not in its proper place. Normally there should be a fold on the dog's ear extending nearly vertically from the bend or fold-over to the lower border, and situated rather behind the middle line of the ear ; and the hang of the ear depends to a great extent on the position of the fold.

To remedy the faulty hang, due either to deficient cartilage or a faulty fold of the ear, there are two recognised methods of treatment, but it will be as well to have a veterinary surgeon to apply them, on the first occasion, at all events.

One plan is to fold the ear and place it as you wish it to hang, and to fasten a weight of lead by means of adhesive plaster on the inside of the fall-over of the ear, so that the ear remains in the position in which it was placed. I have known this method to be successful in small dogs and some dogs of a placid disposition, but I cannot say that I have ever known it to be successful in a Great Dane.

The second plan is to fold the ear in the line of the natural fold from the fall-over to the bottom of the ear, so that the outside or hairy surfaces are together touching, and the under surface is now exposed. While the ear is in this position, a piece of adhesive plaster about an inch broad should be wound tightly (but not so tightly as to stop the circulation) round the ear as close to the line of fall-over—that is, as high up—as possible. This plaster should be left on until it drops off. If the ear then hangs properly, well and good ; if not, another piece should be put on in the same way. It will generally be found that, with young puppies whose ears hang badly owing to a faulty fold, this plan, if not wholly successful, at all events causes marked improvement.

The neck is certainly a very important and most characteristic feature of a Great Dane, and is one that, I am sorry to say, seems to be disappearing in its ideal form. In my opinion, the ears have a great deal to do with a good neck, and formerly, when cropping was permitted, they had a still greater influence, as the healing or cicatrisation of the cropped surfaces contracted the skin, and so drew up that of the neck, making it tight and smooth. " Snake-like " is the adjective applied by the Great Dane Club to the neck when as it should be and I do not think a better description could be found. It should be long, well arched, and quite clean and free from loose skin, well set in the shoulders, while the junction between head and neck should be well defined.

The head and neck combined contribute largely to, if they are not entirely responsible for, the expression which is so important in the Great Dane. I have tried to show which points are entirely dependent on the selection of parents, and which may be modified by human agencies. I am well aware that there are other factors which influence the conformation of some of these points and lest any reader should think I have omitted them, I take this opportunity of saying that they are dealt with in the chapter on " Rearing and Whelping," under which heading they would appear to me to be more appropriately placed.

The shoulders should be muscular, well sloped back and not loaded, while the body and brisket (lower part of chest) should be deep, with the ribs well sprung or arched. This allows plenty of room for the lungs and heart, which, considering the vitality and activity of the breed, is very important. It is a bad fault to have a shallow chest and flat sides, as they suggest want of stamina. While the chest should not be narrow, it should not be very broad when viewed from the front, the room for the lungs being made by the deep brisket and well-sprung ribs. The belly should be well drawn up, and the hindquarters very muscular ; the second thigh should be long and well developed, with the stifle and hock well bent, but turning neither in nor out. These give the suggestion of great power and pace to the dog, and add greatly to the general appearance. The height of the dog at the hindquarters should not be more than it is at the shoulder, as if so it gives a very ungainly form to the dog. The converse is also true, and the dog should not be appreciably shorter at the hindquarters than it is at the shoulder; this type is, on the Continent, described as being of the "hyæna" form.

The tail should be thick at the root and taper to the point. It should not reach much below the hock, or hardly at all. A great many of our dogs have enormously long and enormously thick tails, which is a great pity, as they detract greatly from the possessors' appearance, though a beginner may very likely not appreciate the point. The carriage of the tail is, again, very important. It should be carried low except when in action, when it should be in a line level with the back ; for a dog to carry it arched over the back, or for there to be a marked twist or corkscrew curl in the tail, is a great fault. There should not be, as is often the case, a great amount of hair on the under surface of the tail, which should be attached high up on the hindquarters. It used to be said that the tail should be set on as high as possible, so that when carried horizontally the body and tail made one continuous straight line ; but it has now become fashionable to have the tail set on an inch or so lower, which I am inclined to think is rather to be preferred, though it is in opposition to the German standard. There can be no doubt that the tail being attached in the lower position gives a more graceful finish to the hindquarters than when it is in a straight line with the back.

Feet are, I think, the last point with which I have to deal, having mentioned colour and legs amongst the five cardinal breeding points. These should be round and catlike, well arched, with the toes touching one another, and the nails strong and arched.

I know that one prominent breeder thinks it of no consequence if the feet are hare-like. I, however, entirely disagree with him, as I think that a hare foot very greatly detracts from a Dane's appearance, and I am sure that the great majority of experienced breeders will agree with me. A splay foot in which the toes diverge from one another is even worse than a hare foot, but it can be remedied, as can a hare foot, to a certain slight extent. If your dog develop a splay foot when being kept in a field or on soft ground, the treatment should be taking it for regular walking exercise on a hard road ; if, on the other hand, the splay-footedness shows itself when the dog is kept on an asphalt or hard flooring, two or three handfuls of fine gravel should be thrown on the floor. It will then be found that the dogs will draw up their toes and keep them together so as to prevent the fine gravel getting between them, where it causes considerable irritation if allowed to collect.

I have now referred to all the important desirable points and defects but before leaving this subject I should like to impress on my readers how essential it is that a Great Dane should be symmetrical and well balanced ; every part should be proportionate to its neighbour and the entire animal, so that, taken as a whole, the dog makes a perfect picture which fills the eye and no individual part seems out of harmony.

Some breeders, and even breeders who have had a fair amount of experience, think that it is absurd to attach importance to "general appearance" ; but they are certainly wrong. They think that because their dog has excellent legs, a nice head, a good body and so on, the dog himself must be a magnificent specimen. The various parts of a dog, when examined as such, may be quite good, they may indeed have few if any faults, but when the dog is examined as a whole these parts may be absolutely out of proportion one to another, and this will absolutely spoil the dog as a whole, for it will prevent the appearance of proper balance and harmony.

Becker, in his book on the Great Dane, lays great stress on the dog being symmetrically built, and gives a sketch* with rough comparative measurements. As I think this sketch gives a very good idea of the " balancing " of a Dane, I take the liberty of producing a similar sketch, especially as I think it may be of great help to beginners.

Becker says † that "assuming the dog stands 30in. at the shoulder (line A B) this should be divided into two parts of 15in. each " by a line drawn through E, the junction of elbow and outline of chest ; and that if the height of the hind-quarters is measured by a line drawn through C (the crupper) and the angle of the hips H, the distance CH will be one-third of the whole height C D. Becker also makes the length of the back from A to C equal to the combined length of the dotted lines carried on through the neck and tail from A and C.

*" The Great Dane," F. Becker, p. 83.
†" Op. Cit. Pp. 83-84.

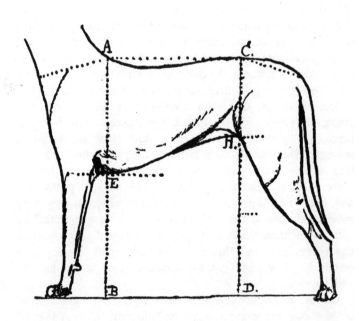

—

CHAPTER V.

Mating, Whelping and Rearing.

Up to the time the bitch is mated with the selected dog, she should lead her ordinary and regular life but it is, of course, of the utmost importance that she should be in as good health as is possible at the time of the mating, and not too fat.

The bitch is usually ready to receive the dog from the tenth to the fourteenth day of her season*; but no hard and fast rule can be laid down, and the best time is when the discharge has become almost colourless, is reduced in quantity, and the swelling is subsiding. If she turn on the dog, snap at him, or tries to sit down, she is generally not ready ; while the signs of sexual excitement which she shows when ready are such as to be unmistakable by the veriest novice.

It has been suggested that there is a difference in the sex of the puppies according to the time at which the bitch is served. For instance, that if the bitch is put to the dog while she is still discharging, the litter contains more bitches than dogs ; and that if the bitch is served at the end of her œstrum, the reverse is the case ; while in the former case the pups resemble the dam, and in the latter the sire. I consider this theory fantastic and quite untrue.

It is always best to muzzle a bitch, and strongly advisable to have her held while being served. If the bitch is not ready, it is she, and not the dog, that should be removed from the place chosen for service, as there is often great

* Even at the very commencement of her season, and before there is any discharge or hæmorrhage, I have known a bitch receive a dog and become pregnant.

43

difficulty in getting away a dog, and especially a big dog. If the dog is much smaller than the bitch, it may be necessary to have some platform on which he can stand.

After mating, the bitch should be allowed to be perfectly quiet for the rest of the day though some fanciers cannot appreciate this important rule ; they will take the bitch a six or seven mile walk to the station immediately after the service, and are surprised when the bitch proves barren. It is best for a bitch that her visit to the dog should extend over two or three days, and that, when possible, a responsible person should accompany her. Some owners of stud dogs give a second service two or three days after the first but one service is quite as effective as several, and from a second service two or three days after the first there arises the danger of a double conception, which, though decidedly rare, should at the same time be considered.

During the period of gestation, which lasts on the average 63 days, the bitch should have plenty of moderate exercise, but it should on no account be excessive or violent. The food should be varied and plentiful, and for the sake of the future puppies the bitch should be given a heaped-up teaspoonful of precipitated phosphate of lime, which is a great bone-making material, or else some preparation of bone meal once a day. About the third, and again about the fifth week, she should be dosed for worms, whether she seems to require it or not, as these pests are the most constant source of early death among puppies. About the sixtieth day she will possibly begin to show signs of uneasiness, and it is as well to give a mild dose of castor oil, and well wash her teats with some good antiseptic.

It does not, of course, follow that because a bitch has been served that she is necessarily in whelp. Mr. Marples has stated that "probably forty per cent. of prize-bred bitches which visit prize-bred dogs are unproductive," for our domesticated dogs lead artificial lives, and we artificially restrict and direct their breeding. The state in which our dogs live is almost entirely artificial in the sense that it differs from what it would be in the wild state. If it was only thoroughly understood that our prize dogs are the result of artificial surroundings, it would do a great deal of good.

44

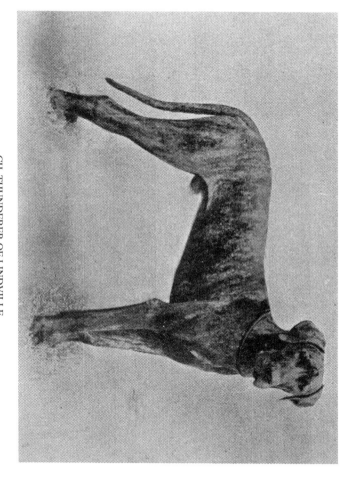

CH. THUNDERER OF LINDVILLE.

CH. CONN OF CLEVELEYS.

Especially is this the case as regards kennelling and feeding, some people thinking that any kennels and any food will do, because they wrongly assume that what is natural is necessarily best. In a wild state dogs would choose their own mates, and the instinct probably remains with them. It has been stated that bitches, while refusing to mate with the dog selected for them, yet show a marked desire for some other dog. I have no personal experience of this, and should doubt it, but at the same time the chances of a good litter are probably greatly increased when inclination is added to opportunity.

Too great a familiarity between the two animals, however, is not to be advised, as a bitch will sometimes refuse a kennel mate with which she has lived and fed since a puppy. The ideal mating would probably be to have three or four selected sires, and to let the bitch choose which she liked ; but this, of course, is beyond the bounds of possibility.

The kennel where the bitch is to whelp should be carefully prepared ; it should be of a fair size, so that there is no possibility of the bitch being cramped for room, and should be light, airy, free from draughts and warm. It should have a thorough " spring cleaning." Everything movable should be taken out and thoroughly washed ; every corner should be scrubbed out with hot water, soda, and some reliable antiseptic. Every particle of old bed and small pieces of straw should be cleaned out ; the floors, doors and walls well scrubbed ; and the kennel left open to air, and thoroughly dry. Warmth in winter can be obtained from a stove, or if this is impossible, buckets of boiling water carefully protected from the bitch will serve in an emergency. As regards the bed to be provided for the whelping bitch, opinions vary greatly, some fanciers believing in a very thick bed of the best wheaten straw, while some go to the other extreme, merely providing a sheet or thick piece of carpet on which the bitch may lie. Those who advocate that the bed should be as thick as possible do so on the grounds that the thick bed obviates all risk of draughts, and also that the puppies can be removed to another portion of the bed, the soiled straw taken away, and fresh layers placed on the foundation, thus obviating the necessity of making up fresh pallets every day

45

and causing the least possible disturbance to the bitch. The reasons against having a thick bed are that the puppies are liable to get hidden in the straw, trodden or lain on, which upsets the bitch, who is already in an excitable and irritable condition. It is undoubtedly true that many bitches will scratch all the straw away and whelp on the bare floor ; but, on the other hand, many bitches will hunt around and deliberately select a big bundle of straw or hay in which to have their family.* Personally, I think that no hard and fast rule can be made, and that it is only by experience that one can tell what is best for any particular bitch. When straw is provided the bitch should be allowed to make her own bed of it, how and where she likes, but it is advisable that she should know the kennel which she is to inhabit, and should have used it before, while it is certainly best that she should be so far removed from the rest of the kennels that the barking and noise which comes from them cause her no disturbance. There should be plenty of water within easy access for the bitch to drink, and on the morning of the sixty-second or evening of the sixty-first day she may be put in the kennel and left as much as possible to herself. It is quite likely that she may refuse food for some hours before the time, but this is no cause for worry.

It is comparatively rarely that Great Danes require human interference during parturition, but they do occasionally, and if there seems to be any difficulty in the puppies being born, or a bitch goes for twelve hours without a further puppy being born (when it is known she has more), a veterinary surgeon should be sent for. It is a sure sign of incipient lunacy for anyone but a veterinary surgeon, or a person of the very greatest experience, to attempt interference or the giving of drugs. The only exception I would make to this rule is where a fancier is living perhaps twenty miles from the nearest surgeon ; but these cases are few and far between, and the owner should find out before-hand what he is to do and how much of any drug he is to give. Occasionally the mother may not be able to sever the umbilical cord, or the puppy may be born with a membrane round it. In these

---

* I know that both Dr. Osburne and Mr. Kirwan use nothing but a sheet or piece of carpet as a bed, but there are other equally experienced breeders who always provide a thick straw bed.

cases the cord may be divided with clean scissors, and the membrane removed with clean fingers. Sometimes, again, we find a puppy motionless and apparently quite lifeless, in spite of the attention bestowed on it by its mother. In a case like this I think the best thing to do is to place a drop or two of brandy upon its tongue, dash a few drops of cold water upon its chest and abdomen—the shock of which will make it take a deep breath,—and then place it before a warm fire, when it will probably soon recover. When all the puppies are born, any dead ones should be removed, and the mother given a bowl of warm milk. It is also as well at this time to examine all the puppies, and see if there are any malformed ones. If there are, they, as well as any mis-coloured ones, should be destroyed at once. It is quite useless to keep merles (blue with black or brindle spots), though this colour was common a hundred years ago, for it is not now a recognised colour ; and equally so to keep brindle-and-whites, brindles with white feet, chests and tails or black-and-whites where the colours are in only two or three different patches. Beginners may find it difficult to believe this statement ; but if they think they can make any money out of these puppies they are greatly mistaken, as they will find to their cost that the price they will receive for such a mismarked puppy will not be equal to the expense of rearing it.

It is worth mentioning that each puppy is attached to the mother by a placenta or after-birth, which is usually born with the puppy, and which the mother almost always eats. I call attention to this because a lot of people think that there is only one placenta for all the puppies, and spend their time, besides being put to needless anxiety, in looking for a large object, which exists only in their imagination.

In anticipation of a possibly numerous litter, all of which it is desired to preserve, a foster-mother should be arranged for, and though I consider one a great nuisance, she is a necessary evil, and the only thing to be done is to minimise the nuisance as much as possible. It is all-important to make arrangements before-hand, as if the supplier is only informed at the last moment, when the foster-mother is actually wanted, it often happens that he is out of stock and

47

wires to someone else, who sends off a bitch which is possibly diseased and most probably has undergone no preparation.

It is most important when the puppies for whom the foster-mother is required are put to her, that her own puppies should be all destroyed, and not a single one left with her. The new puppies should be placed with the foster-mother, well mixed up and left for an hour. By doing this the fresh puppies will acquire the scent of the foster-mother and the foster-mother will, or may, feel a certain amount of discomfort, which will tend to make her take the new puppies more readily. The longer the puppies are kept away from her, the greater of course will be the tendency to take any puppies which will relieve her. If one of her own puppies is given back to the foster-mother, she is almost certain to discriminate between it and the others, and the probability is that she will discard the new puppies and devote all her attention to her own, even going so far as to get away with it on the first possible occasion, and to make a new home, as I have often known happen. For this reason it is essential that none of her own puppies should be left with the forter-mother.

Bitches available as foster-mothers have often been neglected ; they may have the germs of distemper about them or be suffering from mange or worms. At the same time, there are plenty of dealers who will be found reliable, and who can be depended on if a little trouble be taken. It is as well to interview the dealer and the bitch, when by a deposit the bitch can be reserved for you.

It is a far better plan, if possible, to arrange for the use of some bitch which you know in the neighbourhood, and upon which you can keep your eye ; you can then be sure of the time she was served, which should be a few days before your own, and also be certain that she is properly treated for worms, which you can superintend yourself. It is possible by only leaving two or three puppies with the mother, and changing them for another two or three every hour, for one bitch to bring up as many as twelve or thirteen puppies ; but it implies endless trouble and vigilance on the part of her human assistants. I have in this way reared a litter of thirteen puppies ; those that were taken away were fed every hour from the bottle with a mixture of three table-

RUPERT OF RUNGMOOK.

KRISHNA.

spoonfuls of cream and 1¼oz. of Plasmon to a pint of cows' milk, and the result was most satisfactory in every way ; but, as I have already said, this method involves an immense amount of trouble. A much simpler plan is to use the full cream milk powder mentioned in the chapter on " Feeding."* Two and a half ounces of this should be used with half a pint of fresh cow's milk, the powder being gradually mixed with the milk. Some fanciers simply use goat's milk, and there can be no doubt that this answers very well, though personally I prefer the cream milk powder preparation.†

Seven puppies is, as a rule, quite a sufficient number for the mother to rear, though of course she *can* rear more. If a foster-mother is used, it is better that she should be given the smallest puppies, and the best ones reserved for the mother.

On the day after the puppies are born they should be examined for dewclaws, and these should be removed with a pair of sharp curved scissors from both the front and hind legs. Though there is no penalty for dewclaws now, they tend to make a dog cow-hocked, and the back ones are certainly likely to be caught in brambles or in one another, and give rise to a nasty tear. Those on the front leg, though not so noticeable, certainly do not add to the appearance, and as there is no difficulty or pain in removing them, it is better to do so.

The mother will look after the puppies entirely during the first fortnight or three weeks, when they should be taught to lap the mixture of milk, cream, and Plasmon, or milk and cream powder above-mentioned. When a tooth shows they may be started with shredded or the finest minced beef or mutton ; the smallest quantity should be given at first— about a teaspoonful,—which must be gradually increased.‡

While I certainly think that the less the bitch is disturbed during the first week the better, I have never known any harm arise from the visits of her most favoured human

* See page 88.

† It is astonishing that more people do not keep goats for the benefit of their dogs, as without any alteration it will act as an excellent substitute for the bitch's milk. The goat's milk resembles the bitch's more closely than that of any other animal, and two or three milch goats can be bought and kept at the most moderate cost.

‡ Dr. Osburne strongly recommends the giving of raw-meat juice at this age, and his recipe is as follows : Take half a pound of raw beef without fat or gristle, cut it up finely, pour over it a small teacupful of cold water, let it stand in a cool place for three hours, strain through clean muslin, pressing out the juice ; keep quite cold, and give one or two teaspoonfuls three to six times a day.

P

companions. At the same time, I do not advise it except to give food. I am aware that some experienced breeders make it a regular practice to remain with the bitch all through the whelping ; they do it, I believe, for fear of the mother eating or destroying her puppies by lying on them, but in my considerable experience of Great Danes I have never had a case of the former, though I know that it does occasionally occur.

During the third week the puppies should have their claws carefully cut ; they have by this time become very long and sharp, and as the puppies grow they inflict very nasty and painful scratches on their mother unless the claws receive attention. The scratches and abrasions so caused often suppurate, and not only cause considerable pain to the mother—especially when the pups are feeding,—but also the ingestion of the pus and discharge cannot be considered healthy for the puppies.

The subject of puppies' teeth is one that requires careful consideration. The milk teeth can be seen almost as soon as the puppy is born, and are in constant use until the permanent teeth make their appearance, which in a Great Dane is usually from the third month onwards. As the second teeth become prominent, they disturb the milk teeth and loosen them, but it is not advisable to remove the first teeth until they are quite loose, and only then if they come away easily and the gums are inflamed and cause such pain as to make mastication difficult. If they are removed before they are loose, they are not really ready to come away, and their removal is liable to cause malposition of the permanent teeth. At the same time it must be understood that a puppy's mouth requires constant examination from the age of three months until the last permanent tooth has appeared, and if there is any doubt as to there being any misplacement, the puppy should at once be taken to a veterinary surgeon. Beyond the disturbance to the general health caused by inability to eat, as the result of loose teeth and inflamed gums, it is rare to find teething cause much trouble, but it occasionally happens, and especially in an inbred and highly-strung animal, that convulsions may occur, in which case the service of a " vet." should be immediately requisitioned.

The presence of fleas and lice is often the cause of the greatest inconvenience and even suffering to young puppies. It is strange to say so, but I have seen these pests on puppies belonging to most experienced and one would have thought most careful fanciers. Whether they have not been noticed (though I have seen them so thick that they could hardly be missed), or have not been considered of any importance, I do not know, and I would therefore lay stress on the point that it is most necessary to examine young puppies regularly, and that if any fleas or lice are present they should be got rid of at once. The proper treatment, in my opinion, is to wash the dog with soft soap and water, to which has been added Jeyes' fluid in the proportion of a tablespoonful and a half to the gallon. When the dog has been thoroughly washed and dried, an insecticide powder, such as Pyrethrum or sulphur, should be well rubbed into the coat (Keating's powder is another that is easily obtained, and quite efficient). The rubbing-in should be done away from the kennels, so that any insect that has escaped shall not have the opportunity of returning ; this is most important. Another method is to use kerosene and oil (1 to 4), or even common sweet oil with a little oil of anise or sulphur mixed with it.

The kennels, baskets, and everything capable of harbouring a flea, louse, or any parasite should be washed with boiling water and then limewashed. It is quite useless to wash the dogs unless the kennels are also thoroughly cleaned out. The treatment of the dog's coat should be repeated in a few days, so as to make assurance doubly sure.

There is one ailment which pertains to puppies, or at all events young dogs, which for that very reason I think I had better refer to here. Warts are an exceedingly unsightly and to the beginner a very alarming trouble, though, in reality, if properly treated, they need usually cause no anxiety whatever. They most commonly appear in and around the mouth and on the genital organs. Whether they are of exactly the same nature is doubtful, for while the latter are certainly contagious, it is doubtful about the former, though they are probably so and are certainly transmissible by inoculation. These warts appear at times in enormous numbers on and in the mouth of a young Dane, but apart from their unsightliness they do not cause trouble, unless they are knocked or otherwise injured, in which case they bleed very freely, or unless they are in such quantities as to interfere with a dog shutting his mouth or prevent proper mastication, as I have occasionally seen. No treatment is as a rule necessary but if, from one of the causes I have mentioned, operative interference is required, it is essential that a veterinary surgeon should take the matter in hand. The warts bleed so very readily and so copiously that I know of a dog which bled to death when the removal of a large wart on the leg was attempted by an amateur. They almost invariably shrivel up and fall off before the dog attains maturity and I strongly advise any fancier who may have dogs suffering from them to leave them severely alone.*

Lastly, the puppies have to be weaned. I like to begin in the fifth week by taking the mother away for an hour or so, and gradually increasing the time which she spends apart from her puppies ; in this way it is easy to have the weaning completed by the end of the sixth week. Nor must attention to the mother at weaning time be forgotten ; particular care must be observed that the milk is entirely gone before all the puppies are removed. For this purpose it is often advisable to let the smallest and most weakly pups visit their mother two or three times a day after the rest have been permanently removed, otherwise we frequently get trouble from the milk remaining in the gland, and later on fibrous induration of the gland itself, necessitating the use of the surgeon's knife either to open abscesses or to remove tumours and even the gland itself.

A bitch, and especially one that has had two or three litters, may sometimes be found with indrawn nipples. or at all events one or two of them may be so affected, and in such a case it is of course impossible for puppies to use them, If possible, the teat should be drawn out between two fingers, and placed in the puppy's mouth. If this is impossible owing to the shortness of the teat, it can be drawn out in the following manner : An ordinary soda water or lemonade bottle should be dipped into and well rinsed out with hot water.

*Since writing this Mr. Cornish Bowden has told me of a Deerhound which died from starvation and asphyxia. The mouth and back of the throat were covered with warts and it was impossible to operate on account of hæmorrhage.

VENDETTA OF REDGRAVE.

THE GERMAN CHAMPION, TILLY SAULGAU.

It should then be taken out and the neck placed in cold water for about half a minute. The mouth of the bottle should then be placed over the depressed teat, and gently but firmly pressed towards the breast ; as the bottle cools, the teat will be gradually drawn up the bottle, and after remaining in about ten minutes it will generally be found that the teat is long enough for the puppy to take hold of.

It sometimes happens that puppies apparently born well and strong show signs of weakness and diarrhœa during the first twenty-four or forty-eight hours, and if no obvious cause can be found it is quite likely that the dam's milk is at fault. This generally takes the form of excessive acidity, and can easily be verified by the use of a piece of litmus paper. A bitch's milk is normally slightly alkaline, and if so will turn a piece of red litmus paper to a blue colour. If when the litmus paper is placed in contact with the milk it turns or keeps red, there is acidity, and the milk is most unsuitable for the puppies, which should be at once taken away from their mother and fed for the time on the dried cream powder mixture described in the chapter on " Feeding " (page 88). As regards the dam, her milk should be at once drawn off with a breast pump, and she should be given a teaspoonful of bicarbonate of potash in some milk two or three times a day, until the milk again resumes its normal alkaline reaction. " Ashmont "* considers that, apart from excessive acidity, a bitch's milk may sometimes have poisonous or noxious qualities, and from experiments he has made arrives at the conclusion that it is the milk secreted in the first twenty-four hours that has these evil characteristics. He believes that the cause is a physical one, and that it is due to the bitch being nervous and fretful ; personally I do not agree with him, as I think that it is much more likely to be due to errors in feeding.

All—or nearly all—puppies suffer from worms, although they may not be apparent. Worms are certainly the commonest cause of puppy mortality at this age and, whether I know the puppies have them or am in doubt about it, I always make it a rule to treat them at the eighth week. There are various vermifuges—Areca Nut, Santonin, and some of their derivatives, being perhaps the best known—but they

* " Kennel Secrets," p. 275, et seq.

53

should only be given, at all events on the first occasion, in the presence of a veterinary surgeon, and I myself only use them for adult dogs. The one and the only remedy I use for puppies is " Ruby." I consider it infallible and absolutely safe, which is something to be able to say ; as, moreover, full directions are given on the bottles for puppies of all ages and breeds, is is not necessary when using this remedy to have a veterinary surgeon.

This is, perhaps, the best place to mention the points of a puppy which require consideration when selecting one from a litter. There are usually one or two puppies which stand out prominently, but this is not always the case, and occasionally a litter is met with so uniformly good or bad that it is almost impossible to select one as the best. The first point to look for is depth and squareness of the muzzle, and another of almost equal value is a clean, high-carried, well-arched neck. Loose skin about the neck in a puppy I consider is a serious blemish, as my experience teaches me that this tends to increase rather than decrease. Straight legs and big knee joints are important ; and last, but by no means least, the narrower the skull appears in proportion to the muzzle, the better for the future appearance of the dog.

Lastly, I would mention that when the puppies are three months old I separate the dogs from the bitches ; I am quite sure that they do better (though I see no obvious reason in the early months) and grow better—a most important point in rearing good puppies.

CHAPTER VI.

Clubs and Standard of Points,

Until 1903 the Great Dane Club was the only association
in England for the protection and furtherance of the interests
of the breed, and as it was formed in 1882, is by far the oldest
Great Dane club. The original standard was in accord with
that decided on by the principal foreign breeders, at a meeting
held in Berlin in 1880, and the moving spirits of the Club,
when it was started, were Messrs. Frank Adcock, R. Leigh
Pemberton, and Gambier Bolton. In 1894, just before the
Kennel Club passed a rule forbidding the winning of prizes
by any cropped dog (except under certain conditions), the
club decided to dissolve, as the majority of the members
thought it would be useless to have Danes if they were
uncropped. At the moment it certainly seemed as if the
breed had received a blow from which it would never recover,
but there were still some enthusiasts who thought that even
an uncropped Dane was better than none at all, and at the
next Cruft's Show the Club was re-formed on the old lines,
and has flourished with increasing vigour ever since. There
have been three presidents : Lord Lathom, who held office
in the original Club ; Mr. R. Leadbetter, who was elected
president at the reconstitution of the Club, on whose retire-
ment Mr. O. Locker Lampson, M.P., was elected, with Messrs.
F. E. Moss, A. T. Walker, and G. Loder as vice-presidents.
There have been four secretaries :—Mr. del Riego, Mr. Hood
Wright, who held office for nine years, and only relinquished
the post when he left England for Ceylon, Mr. Ernest Fox,
and the present secretary, Mrs. Blackler. The Club has a

number of valuable cups and trophies which are offered for competition as occasion warrants, and, in addition to these cups, the Club gives gold, silver, and bronze medals to all shows where there is a good classification. There are also the Great Dane Breeders' Association, the London and South of England Great Dane Club, the Northern Great Dane Club, and the Scottish Great Dane Club, which cater for the breed in their various districts.

STANDARD OF POINTS.

The Great Dane Club gives the following description of the typical Great Dane, and it is satisfactory to know that all the registered Great Dane clubs have adopted it :—

1. *General Appearance.*—The Great Dane should be remarkable in size and very muscular, strongly though elegantly built ; the head and neck should be carried high, and the tail in line with the back, or slightly upwards, but not curled over the hindquarters. Elegance of outline and grace of form are most essential to a Dane ; size is absolutely necessary ; but there must be that alertness of expression and briskness of movement without which the Dane character is lost. He should have a look of dash and daring, of being ready to go anywhere and do anything.

2. *Height.*—The minimum height of an adult dog over eighteen months must be 30in. ; that of a bitch, 28in.

3. *Weight.*—The minimum weight of an adult dog over eighteen months should be 120lb. ; that of a bitch 100lb.

4. *Head.*—Taken altogether the head should give the idea of great length and strength of jaw. The muzzle or foreface is broad, and the skull proportionately narrow, so that the whole head when viewed from above and in front has the appearance of equal breadth throughout.

The entire length of head varies with the height of the dog, 13in. from the tip of the nose to the back of the occiput is a good measurement for a dog of 32in. at the shoulder. The length from the end of the nose to the point between the eyes should be about equal or preferably of greater length than from this point to the back of the occiput.

The skull should be flat and have a slight indention running up the centre, the occipital peak not prominent. There should be a decided rise or brow over the eyes, but no abrupt stop between them ; the face should be well chiselled, well filled in below the eyes with no appearance of being pinched ; the foreface long, of equal depth throughout. The cheeks should show as little lumpiness as possible compatible with strength.

(a) *Lips.*—The lips should hang quite square in front forming a right angle with the upper line of foreface.

(b) *Underline.*—The underline of the head, viewed in profile, should run almost in a straight line from the corner of the lip to the corner of the jawbone, allowing for the fold of the lip, but with no loose skin to hang down.

(c) *Jaw.*—The teeth should be level and not project one way or the other.

(d) *Nose and Nostrils.*—The bridge of the nose should be very wide, with a slight ridge where the cartilage joins the bone. (This is quite a characteristic of the breed). The nostrils should be large, wide, and open, giving a blunt look to the nose. A butterfly or flesh-coloured nose is not objected to in harlequins.

(e) *Ears.*—The ears should be small, set high on the skull, and carried slightly erect with the tips falling forward.

5. *Neck.*—The neck should be long, well arched, and quite clean and free from loose skin, held well up, snakelike in carriage, well set in the shoulders, and the junction of head and neck well defined.

6. *Shoulders.*—The shoulders should be muscular but not loaded, and well sloped back, with the elbows well under the body.

7. *Forelegs and Feet.*—The forelegs should be perfectly straight, with big bone. The feet should be catlike, the toes well arched and close, the nails strong and curved.

8. *Body.*—The body should be very deep, with ribs well sprung and belly well drawn up.

9. *Back and Loins.*—The back and loins should be strong, the latter slightly arched.

10. *Tail.*—The tail should be thick at the root, and taper towards the end reaching to or just below the hocks. It

should be carried, when the dog is in action, in a straight line level with the back, slightly curved towards the end, but in no case should it curl or be carried over the back.

11. *Hindquarters.*—The hindquarters and thighs should be extremely muscular, giving the idea of great strength and galloping power. The second thigh is long and well developed, the stifle and hock well bent, the hocks set low, turning neither out nor in.

12. *Coat.*—The hair is short and dense and sleek looking, and in no case should it incline to roughness.

13. *Movement.*—The action should be lithe, springy, and free. The hocks move freely, and the head be carried high except when galloping.

14. *Colour.* (*a*) *Brindles.*—Brindles must be striped. Ground colour from the lightest yellow to deep orange, and the stripes must always be black.

(*b*) *Fawns.*—The colour varies from lightest buff to deepest orange, darker shadings on the muzzle and ears and around the eyes are by no means objectionable.

(*c*) *Blues.*—The colour varies from light grey to deepest slate.

(*d*) *Blacks.*

In all the above colours white is only admissible on the chest and feet, but is not desirable even there. The nose is always black (except in blues). Eyes and nails preferably dark.

(*e*) *Harlequins.*—Colour pure white underground with preferably black patches (blue patches permitted), having the appearance of being torn. In this variety wall eyes, pink noses, or butterfly noses are not a fault.

CHAPTER VII.

Great Dane Type.

At the end of 1925 some very interesting correspondence appeared in " Our Dogs " concerning the type question. I take the liberty of re-printing below the more important of these letters :—

" Very many old Dane breeders have disappeared since the war, and, to my mind, there is a great danger of the true conception of Dane type disappearing with them.

" The ' Standard of Points ' lays down that ' the Great Dane should be remarkable in size and very muscular . . . elegance of outline and grace of form are essential . . . size is absolutely necessary . . . alertness of expression and briskness of movement, without which the true Dane character is lost . . . a look of dash and daring, of being ready to go anywhere and do anything.'

" A few of our present Danes certainly fulfil these conditions and appear consistently in your show criticisms ; but many others attain exalted positions, though one cannot reconcile their appearance with the above description. This gives rise to many erroneous ideas concerning Dane type. I have even been assured on one occasion that great size is now unnecessary, and have frequently heard particularly well-muscled-up dogs described as ' loaded in shoulder.'

" ' Size is essential.' But ' quality,' as described above, is equally necessary. Tall, flat-sided dogs, noticeably lacking in muscle and stamina, are unworthy of the title ' Great Dane,' and, indeed, their demeanour often indicates no readiness ' to go anywhere,' except on a leash ; whilst their self-confidence to ' do anything ' has too obviously been curtailed by the consistent use of that leash, doubtless occasioned by the fond anxiety of their doting owners.

59

" A wide skull undoubtedly denotes coarseness, and coarseness is not in keeping with the Standard of Points. Yet several dogs with very coarse skulls have recently achieved premier honours. At the same time, length of head only, without width and depth of foreface, together with lack of ' chisel,' is inconsistent with the ' look of dash and daring ' that is required. Yet many dogs appear to be judged on head merely by mathematical proportion of length.

" Again, ' hackney action ' (waving his legs in the air before placing them in approximately the same spot from which they were removed) is unsuitable in a dog claiming descent from the Boarhound. The latter's *raison d'etre* must have called for a low, sweeping stride, with the hind feet brought well forward (not up), to give length of stride and consequent speed in overtaking his quarry. Yet high (and, therefore, somewhat stitled) action appears to be popular, and can usually be attained by a further judicious (?) use of the leash.

" To my mind the correct standard is clear. Size without coarseness but with an appearance of ' breeding,' vitality, pluck, and power, is required, the Dane being, in the canine species, a replica of the best class of weight-carrying hunter in the equine. Yet it is only too noticeable that many dogs now successful in the show ring could not fulfil these conditions ; whilst many others, fully capable of showing true Dane character, are reduced by lack of proper training and handling to the level of flaccid-muscled, drowsy-eyed, Brobdingnagian lap-dogs.

H. A. U. D. MENDAX." (Mrs H. M. Cowan.)

" I also think the time has come when Great Dane type should be laid down, and adhered to.

" Take the three winning dogs in any class, and in the majority of cases they have no resemblance to each other in any way, either in size, type, or soundness, that one wonders how the judge places them.

" Some of the present-day Danes stand in the ring resembling the old cab horse one used to encounter at the

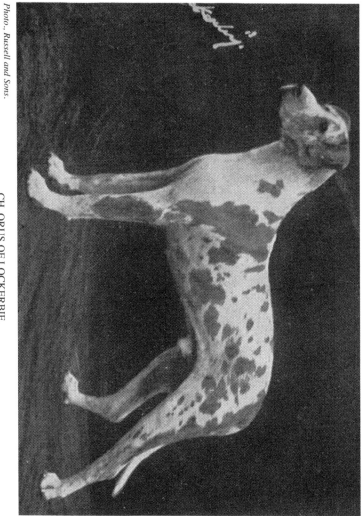

CH. ORUS OF LOCKERBIE.

Photo., Fall.

CH. IOMAR OF LOSEBERY.

London railway stations before the introduction of taxis—over at the knees, as if they are waiting for their last day to come,—and one often sees these noble dogs, who should look (according to one of our greatest authorities on dogs) that they only let other dogs live by their sufferance, having to have toy bunny rabbits, indiarubber squeakers, etc., pushed under their noses to try and get them to show their expression. No dog can show any expression if they have no stop, which is lacking in our present-day Danes, and one can imagine the lord of the manor starting out for a day's wild boar hunting with twenty of the present-day dogs. I think it would become a case of the hunter becoming the hunted.

"They have no comparison with the breed as laid down by the rules and points of the Great Dane Club Book, and to my mind this is entirely the fault of the Great Dane Club, who have a committee of twelve, 75 per cent. of which put in the grand total attendance of 0, and then offer their services for re-election.

"I think the time has come to express the opinion of a well-known breeder, that what is wanted is a Great Dane Breeders' Association. One that will look after the breed and see that this once noble dog does not degenerate any further.

W. C. JARVIS."

"As a breeder and exhibitor of Great Danes for over 20 years, I have been interested in reading the letters in your paper on 'Great Dane Type.' Mr. Mendax (who I am not acquainted with as a Great Dane breeder) is quite correct in stating that the true conception of a Great Dane is being lost. In all descriptions of the breed the necessity of great size is emphasized. It is comparatively easy to breed a quality small dog ; it is far more difficult to breed a sound quality large dog—but how one is repaid when one does. The Dutch judge at the last Cruft's Show was of this opinion.

"As regards heads, many breeders to whom I have lately talked, regret as much as I do the lack of wrinkle, stop, well filled-up foreface—the look of power and intelligence. The mania for very narrow, long heads will pay its own penalty ;

in a generation or two the offspring of these dogs will be decidedly snipy and weak in foreface, and lack the square muzzle without which a Dane loses its character. The breeding of Danes was chiefly in the hands of comparative novices—all praise to them for doing their best—but, unfortunately, they have not in the back of their minds the remembrance of the splendid types of the breed that filled the ring in pre-war days.

" The type of foreface that one wants to keep is that of Ch. Thunderer, depicted in the late Dr. Morell Mackenzie's book on the Great Dane—a typical, powerful, intelligent foreface, denoting the strength a Great Dane should have. Again, a head must be in proportion to the size of the dog. To quote Dr. Morell Mackenzie : ' It used to be considered that the longer and leaner a Dane's head, the better it was, but this is not the case. A head which measured 13½in. from occipital protuberance to tip of nose would be quite out of place in a dog measuring 31in. at the shoulder, as it would be out of all proportion as regards length—being much too long ; and a *Great Dane must, before everythivg, be symmetrical and properly balanced.* Nor are size and power in the head necessarily synonymous with coarseness, as some people seem to think. The cheeks should not be perfectly flat, but should show development—absolute flatness would denote non-development of the masseter or cheek muscle, and signify an absence of power.' Herr Gustav Fang writes : ' A dog with flat cheeks has lost the character of a Great Dane.'

" To my mind, the worst faults of the present-day Great Dane is the lack of really good body properties, the terrible hindquarters, and the amount of loose skin in the neck. If I had a dog with a really loose-skinned neck I should certainly not show it, and until breeders set themselves a higher standard these faults will persist. I should advise all breeders and judges to thoroughly ' chew and digest ' Dr. M. Mackenzie's book on the Great Dane. He was a great judge of the breed, and a scientific one as well.

" One has to allow a great deal for the ' temperament ' of the breed. Many Danes, especially those who lead a natural life and are perfectly alert and full of go at home, resent being on a leash at a show, and make the most of themselves. But, still, even a want of alertness in the ring cannot debar what good points they have.

" Mr. Jarvis allows his enthusiasm for the breed to run away with his good sense when he blames the committee of the Great Dane Club for Danes not reaching the correct standard as laid down in the club rules. Does he expect the committee to approach different breeders and say : ' Look here, we don't approve of the type you breed ; you must alter your tactics and breed something better.' The committee is composed chiefly of old and experienced breeders who desire the welfare of the breed as much as Mr. Jarvis does. It is up to every breeder who is a member of the Great Dane Club to abide by its rules and to conform to the standard of points laid down for the breed by the club.

" Judging is not quite such an easy task as Mr. Jarvis seems to think. It is true that the three winning dogs in any class may be of quite distinct types, but judged on the merits of the ' whole dog ' they are probably the ' three best,' but one may excel in head, and have a bad neck ; the second may excel in neck, have a medium head, and a well-formed body ; the third might have everything about it excellent but fail in head to the others ; hence the different types, and hence the necessity of a really experienced judge.

" The future of the breed lies entirely in the hands of exhibitors, and until they take sufficient pride in showing only dogs that are perfectly sound and without any glaring and pronounced faults, the breed will deteriorate, but to do this the breeding stock must be of the very best, especially the bitches. Every brood bitch should be up to the highest show form ; from her earliest puppyhood she should be fed on the most nourishing foods, chiefly meat, and she should have a pedigree behind her of equally good ancestors.

" No dog need be unsound ; no dog need have bad hind-quarters, nor a loose-skinned neck, nor lack of muscle, nor if properly managed need they be non-breeders. So many people forget that a Great Dane is a ' hunting hound,' and should be kept in as hard condition as a Foxhound. I am quite sure that every Dane in my kennel would take the greatest pleasure in tackling a wild boar.

" What I really should like to know is whether a Dane constitutionally unsound should be allowed to win at all. No unsound horse in a show ring would pass the judge.

" HILDA STARK."

" *Re* the allegations against my committee, I would point out that this body is elected by general vote of the members of the Club, and it is, therefore, entirely in their own hands whom they choose to represent them. It is also open to any member to offer him- or her-self for election to the committee, of which privilege Mr. Jarvis does not appear to have availed himself.

" In justice to the Club, of which I have the honour to be secretary, I claim that the present increasing popularity of the breed is largely owing to its efforts. The Club very gallantly came to the rescue after the war, and in spite of many difficulties, financial and otherwise, ensured that the breed was represented at the shows, and did everything in its power to assist breeders, whether members or otherwise.

" My committee welcomes any honest criticism, and if our members have any further grievances to bring forward I shall be greatly obliged if they will do so. If brought to the light of day they may prove to be as fallacious as those of Mr. Jarvis.

" I entirely agree with Mr. Jarvis and with H. A. U. D. Mendax, in his letter in your October 16 issue, *re* the difference in type of the present-day Great Danes. This makes a judge's task a very difficult one, and probably accounts for the many criticisms levelled at the judging. It must be remembered, however, that owing to the difficulty of breeding during the war, and the resulting shortage of dogs, it was impossible for breeders to proceed on scientific lines, and breed from those strains which they would select had they a wider choice. It takes many generations to re-establish a type, but this matter

CH. FORTUNA OF LOCKERBIE.

FIGARO OF ST. AUSTELL.

is now rectifying itself, and from the number of promising young dogs and puppies I have seen lately, I think it is probable that we shall again see the pre-war standard in our show rings.

S. MAY BLACKLER, Hon. Sec.,
The Great Dane Club."

" Mr. Jarvis is wrong in assuming that Great Dane type is not laid down. It is, and very clearly so, in the Great Dane Club Book. That it is not adhered to is due principally to faulty selection of breeding-stock, caused either by ignorance or misplaced economy. By the latter, I mean using second-rate stud dogs standing at a slightly lower fee than some of those true to type, or using a worthless dog in one's own kennel. Consequently (with all respect to the opinion of one of your ' Great Dane Growlers,' in your issue of October 16) very few really typical Danes are now to be seen in this country.

" A second-rate dog is rarely profitable to his owner, and is most detrimental to the breed. By ' second-rate ' I mean an untypical dog with hereditary faults. A dog unsuitable (or handicapped) for the show ring by reason of injuries or non-hereditary complaints (amongst which I include weakness in fore- but not in hind-legs), but otherwise sound and typical, is often a very desirable stud dog. In connection with this I hold that the sire is far more likely to pass on unsoundness than the dam.

" ' Stop ' is certainly lacking in many Danes ; but it is the longitudinal indentation, running between the eyes up to the skull, and the raised eyebrows, rather than ' stop,' that is necessary to give the ' frown,' so characteristic of true Dane expression.

" Mr. Jarvis's simile of the ' old cabhorse . . . over at the knees ' is unhappy, inasmuch that it is far preferable for a Hound to be ' over ' than ' back ' at the knees. Some of our best Danes have stood a trifle ' over ' when not alert.

" Since time immemorial various devices have been adopted to make dogs alert in the ring. It is even stated (probably not on the best authority) that the Lady Eve attributed her

G

success in the open class at the Eden K.C. show to the use of a ' squeaker,' whittled by Adam for his offspring, and snatched from the latter when his mother's Boarhound, Marvellous Miracle, failed to respond to the lure of an apple (also snatched). Though, personally, I have always held that the sudden alertness that won ' Miracle ' his first certificate was caused rather by the consequent uproar from the despoiled Abel at the ringside. Alertness can usually be better achieved by training a Dane to look for his owner (lurking outside the ring whilst a friend does the handling) than by the use of ' lures.'

' I cannot pass over Mr. Jarvis's attack on the Great Dane Club. He appears to hold the club (or its committee) responsible for the faulty methods of breeders ! The club has laid down an excellent and considered ' Standard of Points,' and can hardly be blamed if breeders are failing at present to produce dogs consistent with that standard.

" I do not understand Mr. Jarvis's differentiation between the ' Great Dane Club ' and a ' Great Dane Breeders' Association.' It is certainly regrettable that more members of the committee are not able to attend the meetings regularly, but I think the quota able to do so is more likely to effect the furtherance of the breed's interest than any (shall I say?) system of Soviet government. After all, there is at least one general meeting yearly at which all members of the club are asked to be present, and at which the proportional attendance is far below that of an average committee meeting.

" Whilst it is surely reasonable that only those breeders who have proved themselves competent as judges should be put on the club's list of judges, one may safely assume that the committee would enable anyone who had proved himself capable of breeding and rearing Danes of the right type to qualify for this list by suggesting his name as judge at a minor show, although he had not judged previously.

" Improvement in Great Dane type is not to be achieved by pointless criticism of the Great Dane Club, but by more intelligent attention to the selection of breeding-stock and

66

to better training methods on the part of breeders and owners.

H. A. U. D. MENDAX."

" I am pleased to see the correspondence *re* the above. I agree with Mr. Jarvis, the standard laid down by the specialist clubs should be adhered to, and that several of our winning Danes to-day are far from sound. Many of the judges think head is all that is required. and forget that soundness, in any animal, should come first. In our Danes, we also want size without coarseness, and he must be alert.

" Our Danes to-day are practically up to pre-war standard· The London and South of England Great Dane Club, while the other Great Dane Clubs closed down, during the war, and after, did all that was possible to keep the breed from deteriorating, and thanks are due to the committee and members of this club, who were all breeders, that the Dane is what it is to-day.

" I quite agree with previous writers that scientific breeding is necessary, but when judges place as winners unsound dogs, it places everyone, especially the novices, in a quandary what to breed for. Judges must be asked to judge according to the standard laid down, and then with scientific breeding we shall keep the breed from degenerating. I agree with Miss Stark, soundness is most essential, and ' no unsound horse in a show ring would pass the judge ; then, why a dog ?

EDA KINSMAN YOULDEN,
Hon. Secretary, London and South of England
Great Dane Club."

" I have read with great interest the recent letters published in *Our Dogs re* Great Dane type. I have only been breeding Danes since the war, but I think I am at liberty to give my opinion against older breeders. We are told that the ' standard of points ' to· aim at are those drawn up by the Great Dane Club. Miss Stark has written us a very good letter on these points. Everyone will admit that many of the Danes seen in the ring at the recent championship shows are almost a disgrace to the breed. Many of these were owned and exhibited by some of our oldest breeders. If these people, to whom we ought to be able to look for good specimens and advice as to how to breed them, show dogs which we moderns would be ashamed to show or have in our kennels, what respect can we have for their methods?

" The judges at the recent championship shows are all old breeders, and should, therefore, know better than anyone what is a good Dane—*i.e.*, conforms with the standard laid down. We are told that ' elegance of outline and grace of form are the most essential points of a Dane ' a thing which no Dane can have unless he is sound. How many of the recent winners can be called ' elegant ' ? How many of them are perfectly sound? What is the use of the members of the Great Dane Club committee telling us that theirs is the true Dane standard if, when they themselves judge, they award the prizes to a totally different type of Dane?

" Why cannot the list of points or marks laid down by the club be used by the Great Dane Club judges when judging? If this list is not considered to be put down in the best possible manner, then let each judge make his own list before judging and award the dogs he has under him so many marks for each point. And then let each exhibitor be told which points his dog has lost marks on and where he has gained. In this way even an absolute novice would know where he was and what to aim at in breeding. I think something of this sort ought to be put before the Great Dane Club at their next general meeting.

A New Daneite."

" I expressed an opinion that the only hope of breeding really high-class puppies was to use only brood bitches of the greatest quality and up to the best show form. I have since come across a book on dogs, published more than twenty years ago, in which the account of the Great Dane is written by Mrs. Horsfall. I was immensely interested to see she held the same opinion. She writes : ' It is useless to try to breed a show Great Dane from anything except very high-class parents. It seems that in other breeds a bitch, providing she is well bred and is judiciously mated, may breed champions.

CH. ZENDA OF SUDBURY.

RUBINA OF RUNGMOOK.

This is not so with Great Danes, save in a very few exceptional cases. In fact, unless the dam herself were good in show points, it would not be worth troubling to breed from her—that is, if any high-class progeny were expected.' It is on this point that so many new breeders come to grief ; either they make the fatal mistake of indiscriminately purchasing several second-rate dogs, or they buy (often at a ridiculously large price) a bitch that under no circumstances will ever breed anything worth having. For anyone starting a kennel my advice is : Let them put all their money into the best bitch they can buy ; get the advice of a really experienced breeder as to what dog to mate her to, and then build up their kennel from the resulting progeny. It is far more satisfactory and gives far more pleasure to breed one's own winners, and is far more creditable.

" I do not agree with Mr. Mendax that the stud dog placed at the highest fee is necessarily the best dog to use ; the amount of a fee is simply the value set on the use of the dog by its owner.

" The reason so many Danes have bad and undeveloped hindquarters is, I think, due to the totally inadequate size of their kennels. The ideal housing for Great Danes are ordinary loose horse-boxes. Failing these, it is not a very expensive job to erect timber ones ; in fact, they can be built at a lower cost than many of the ordinary kennels are sold at.

" Many people are so afraid of giving too much meat. For generations my dogs have been fed nearly entirely on meat, and to this I put down their immunity from distemper. None of my adult dogs have had that dread disease, nor have any of my bitches failed to breed. I believe that many bitches go wrong when whelping because it is the custom at these times to feed with various sloppy foods, which the average dog always digests with difficulty.

HILDA STARK."

" The late Dr. Morell Mackenzie in his book ' Great Danes, Past and Present,' in his preface states, ' That it is only now, thirty-two years to the day since I had my first Dane, that I am beginning to hope I have learned something.' Words like this coming from such a great authority on the breed, makes one wish we only had such a man now to correct our faults ; and what an ideal for breeders and judges to live up to !

" Miss Stark's letter is very interesting, inasmuch as she admits the type is not what it was both regarding character in head, body properties, etc., and also states that the breeding was in the hands of comparative novices, who have not had the experience of knowing the pre-war dogs.

" Quoting from Dr. Morell Mackenzie, the same chapter as Miss Stark, page 46, he says, ' For a long while, in fact, until quite recently a good head seemed the be all and end all of a Great Dane's qualifications, and if the dog only possessed a good long narrow head, many judges seemed quite oblivious to the importance of body, legs, neck, or anything else,' and states that Dr. Sidney Turner has pointed out, ' The head is a sort of fifth limb.' Now if the present mania for heads is still going on and Miss Stark admits it is, and ' Great Danes, Past and Present,' was published in 1912, the present-day comparative novice could not be blamed for that, and I maintain that after the war the novices had to get their stock from the fortunate breeders who were able to retain them during the war period, so that to my mind the present-day Dane is the offspring of that stock. Then again, who makes the type- Not the novice by any means. It's the judges who are all old and experienced breeders, and if they choose to give an award to a dog with a long narrow head, no stop or chiselling, and bad body properties, one can hardly blame the novice. They use the prize-winners to improve their stock.

" I certainly agree with Miss Stark that an unsound dog should not win a prize, yet they do, and sound typical dogs are sent way cardless.

" As regards the committee of the Great Dane Club, I still maintain that it is their duty to see the rules of the club carried out. Rule 2 states ' the objects of the Great Dane Club are to improve the breed of Great Danes and to make the qualities and type of the breed better known, to define precisely and publish a description of the same, and to urge the adoption of such type upon breeders, judges, and exhibitors as the recognised standard by which Great Danes are to be judged.' It might be too blunt to say to this or that breeder, you must not breed to so-and-so type, but we have a column in *Our Dogs* every week where, diplomatically, breeders, judges, and novices could be told. The column is free and is for items of interest, and that to my mind is the mouthpiece of the breed.

" Why I have never availed myself of the opportunity to serve on the committee, is, because I knew in my own mind I should not always be able to attend their meetings, and rather than become an ornament instead of an assistant, I have refrained from putting up my name for election. Unfortunately, I am not a gentleman of leisure.

" Going back to Dr. Morell Mackenzie's book, I should like to state here that his chapter on ' Dont's ' for exhibitors at shows is well worth reading and inwardly digesting, and the same applies to his advice to judges, as it is quite evident, that what happens to-day happened then.

W. C. JARVIS."

CHAPTER VIII.

Colour Breeding.

The question of colour keeps cropping up, so the following will be a guide to many. Brindles should be striped ; ground colour from the lightest yellow to deep orange, and the stripes must always be black. Fawns.—The colour varies from lightest buff to deepest orange, darker shading on the muzzle and ears, and around the eyes are by no means objectionable. Blues.—The colour varies from light grey to deepest slate. In all the above colours and black, white is only admissible on the chest and feet, but is not desirable even there. The nose is always black (except in blues) ; eyes and nails preferably black. Harlequins.—Colour pure white underground, with preferably black patches (blue patches permitted), having the appearance of being torn. In this variety wall eyes, pink noses, and butterfly noses are not a fault.

Re the breeding of harlequins, the following is quoted from a letter written by Mrs Cowan (née Dickinson) who must have bred as many harlequins as most of the present-day breeders :—

" I believe it has always been recognised that a black or blue should be crossed in about every third generation to avoid harlequins being too lightly marked. Figaro of St. Austell, Ch. Zena of Sudbury, my own Rebel of Rungmook, and her brother and sister, Sunstar and Ch. Stella of Seisdon, are examples of well-known harlequins bred by a black dog out of a harlequin bitch. Rebel and Stella were, however, blue-and-white, not black-and-white, although there was no blue ancestor for several generations back. Ch. Iomar of Losebery, Ch. Fortuna of Lockerbie, and Ch. Minka de Grace were by a harlequin dog out of a black bitch. Ch. Zenda of Sudbury, Ch. Shikari of Bellary, Lady Vanity, and Ch. Gloria of Breamore are examples of successful harlequin-to-harlequin mating, though Gloria's sire, Ch. Orus of Lockerbie, was a brindle-harlequin, in the days when such a colour was permissible.

" I consider a harlequin dog to a merle bitch one of the best matings, and, so far as I can remember, Leta of Taperow and Lady of Portswood were by a harlequin dog out of a bitch which, though classified as a harlequin, was actually a merle.

" The best harlequin dog I have ever seen was out of the same dam by a harlequin sire, and was shown by Mr. Clifford Slack at our Club show under a German judge. The judge's idea of a Dane was, in my opinion, unusual—to say the least of it,—and he put him below many unsound and in every way inferior dogs, though I considered him better than my Ch. Rupert, who was preferred to him by the judge. Mr. Slack, I believe, was so disgusted that he sold the dog to America, on an offer he already had, and I have always regretted that such a beautiful dog was lost to the breed in this country.

" The breeding, blue to harlequins, is also useful, the resulting harlequin puppies usually being black-and-white, and not blue-and-white, as one might expect. In fact, Miss Battle tells me her harlequin bitch, Seamere Survivor, produced eight such harlequins out of a litter of 12 by my blue dog, Roland.

" I have four harlequin bitches in my kennel at present, two being black-and-white and two blue-and-white ; but my recent experience of getting such a large proportion of mismarks from mating harlequin to harlequin has decidedly influenced me in favour of one parent being blue, black, or merle. One further point may be useful to novices : I have always found that a black bitch mismarked with white on legs, face, etc., is useless for breeding harlequins, though she is likely to throw whole-colour puppies to a blue or black dog."

Mrs. Blackler is, however, inclined to dispute Mrs. Cowan's statement that a mismarked black bitch is useless for harlequin breeding. as some of the best harlequins she ever bred were out of a black bitch with a white blaze and white on her neck and feet ; but she was by the famous Figaro of St. Austell out of a harlequin-bred black bitch. Mrs. Blackler thinks it is not so much the colour of the sire and dam, but that of the preceding generations, that should be considered; though even then there are surprises, as she once had a beautiful golden-brindle puppy from a sire and dam who had been harlequin and black bred for generations.

Mrs. Napier Clavering's experience in breeding brindles is that it is absolutely necessary to use a black Dane occasionally, otherwise she finds breeding brindle with brindle continuously, or sometimes a fawn, that the stripes in time get few and far between. She is absolutely dead against using blues or harlequins with either brindles or fawns, as that leads to mismarked puppies. If a black has been carefully bred with good brindle or fawn blood, all brindle and fawn on one side and some on the other, the result is usually well-marked puppies.

With regard to Mrs. Blackler's golden-brindle puppy from harlequin and black breeding, the Hon. W. B. Wrottesley bred a golden-brindle, whole brother to Seignor of Seisdon, a black, strongly harlequin-bred—but most Danes, even harlequins, have a distant brindle ancestor somewhere—Ch. Viceroy of Redgrave in most cases. Mrs. Cowan says that a dark-brindle occurs more frequently than a golden-brindle in harlequin-bred litters, and only lately a dark-brindle bitch of strong harlequin breeding (Ch. Shikari ex Gazara) was mated to her Roland, and the resulting litter reverted to ancestry, and the puppies were black and harlequin.

Regarding the mating of other colours, the following is Mrs. Cowan's view on the subject, and her "tips" may be useful to beginners. "Brindle to brindle should not be repeated for more than about two generations without crossing in a fawn, or the puppies are likely to become too dark in colour. If fawn and fawn is repeated too often without crossing in a brindle, the puppies may be too washy in colour. Black to brindle is usually inadvisable, as most blacks are harlequin-bred, and brindled harlequins and merles may result. Blue to blue can be repeated indefinitely. Blue to brindle or fawn usually produces blacks (often rusty blacks in the latter case)."

Concerning the subject of colour-breeding, Mr. Geo. Horowitz has recently written an article for the Press which I have pleasure in including in this work. It is as follows :—

74

" I have recently been looking over some last year's copies of the German canine journal *Hundesport und Jagd*, one of which contained an article on the breeding of Great Danes, by Herr Paul Schneider, of Homburg. Shortly afterwards I chanced on some remarks relating to the above article, remarks made by the well-known Swiss Great Dane fancier, Mr. C. H. Baltischwiler, in the *Schweizer Hundesport und Jagd*. His observations (with which I quite agree) refer to the present status of the breed in Switzerland, and may, to a certain extent, be also applied to the Great Danes in this country.

" Great Danes are a variety that has greatly suffered through the war, at least in England, and there are, unfortunately, not a few representatives with large skulls, heavy cheeks, long bodies, light eyes, and bad colour, but, thanks to some good recent importations from Germany, the way for our Great Dane Breeders should be clear enough, because it is not for the judge to do this, as the imported specimens, being cropped, cannot be exhibited for competition. However, it is very important for the Great Dane Club to act as early as possible and restore the Great Dane to the elevated position it held before the war.

" Breeding Great Danes to type is not such an easy matter as it would seem. Breeders should note that in Germany the breeding of Great Danes is on similar blood-lines to the breeding of Alsatians, and this is an answer to the question that is often being put to me as to what German breeders do to obtain such beautiful necks in their Danes. The important thing, therefore, is to breed Great Danes on blood-lines. In other words, it is not the parents only, but the ancestors which should be considered, and the more quality ancestors there are in the pedigree the greater the expectation that the puppies may resemble the forefathers known to the breeder— *i.e.*, that they may remain of the same type. To obtain this result one has recourse to in-breeding—*i.e.*, nearly related stock is crossed together which originates from the same ancestors, and possessing as few faults as possible, but in type differs as much as possible, and which have been bred in different surroundings and differently fed. The latter point, in my opinion, is not without importance. Two Great

Danes that have been reared and kept under different conditions of life should possess less defects in common, defects which may be due to the mode of rearing and feeding, than those which live in the same kennel and under the same conditions. Of course, it is presumed that the Great Dane breeder conforms to the exigencies of the standard in every respect—viz., size, quality, bone, and strength. It is also necessary to attend to the colour question in addition to that of good health, strength, and soundness. Only strong colours should be used in breeding Great Danes. The progeny of the light golden-brindle or fawn grandparents of a pale colour, white markings, lightly coloured nails, and, especially, light eyes, should not be used. This last point is of great importance. A Great Dane with yellow-amber eyes, or with eyes of pale green-yellow colour that are at present often met with, and which remind one of gooseberry jelly, are abominable. In breeding brindle-and-fawn Great Danes we must always follow the old-established rule, which is to mate brindles with fawns, and if the brindle colour is not a light-brindle, the mating as above will balance the pigment in such a manner that the fawn will not become too light and the brindle not too dark. In other words, the colours of the ancestors will be maintained. The parent-stock which is bred constantly from the same strain transmits its properties in a more reliable form, because fewer ancestors make their influence felt than animals which do not originate from a related stock, and this may go so far that, for instance, a Great Dane dog which constantly figures in the pedigree of his strain has an influence not only by himself, but also through the blood of fewer ancestors that has accumulated and become stronger in him, and this to such a degree that even the progeny sired by him out of a less valuable bitch is good, and, as a rule, transmits the good qualities of the ancestors of the dog and not of the bitch. However, if we breed from stock which is called 'chance stock,' the progeny, even if we again use a very typical stud dog, will very often exhibit the defects of the granddam. To sum up, in breeding Great Danes it is not only the parents, but the grandparents, that should be taken into account in mating, and through mating suitably related animals one should create a fixed strain ; but Great

PORTHOS OF ESPERANCE.

Photo., Fall.

REMUS MENIEL VON HORST.

Danes without coarse faults should be used, and only those which answer the requirements of the standards. The very best are just good enough, and on no account should one breed with Great Danes which are not sound and healthy or possess anatomical defects—rickets, uneven teeth (overshot or undershot), etc. Great Dane puppies should be reared with their freedom, and breeders must not only look after the 'tummy' of their dogs, but also after their mental development, the Great Dane being an extraordinary grateful animal.

"A Great Dane which is destined to pass its life in a kennel is to be pitied, for the prominent qualities of the breed suffer thereby. They are essentially companion dogs, and develop in a splendid manner in the midst of human beings, and belong to those breeds which are invaluable as guards for the house and yard, and it is quite unnecessary—and, as a matter of fact, not to be recommended—to train a Great Dane. A young Great Dane grows up imperceptibly and absolutely independently to the conditions of its household, and fulfils its task as guard and companion by itself, and without any bother on the part of its master. Given good and reasonable treatment, they are not only handsone but also good and in all circumstances reliable friends. The old saying that 'everybody has the dog which he deserves' can be well applied to the Great Dane.

"Judging by what we meet at shows, we possess in England black-and-white, brindle, fawn, black, and blue Great Danes. However, there are at the present moment very few fawns, still fewer blues, and still less blacks. If I am not mistaken the blue variety used to be very fashionable in this country shortly before the war, and I know that there are a few Great Dane breeders in England who are very keen on this colour, but they seem to be rather perplexed as to how to obtain it, and I think, therefore, that a few words on this question will be of use to them. It is the same case in Germany, where, according to my old friend the secretary of the German Great Dane Club, the blue variety of Great Danes is called 'our step-child,' and the above great authority puts the question in the German canine journal, *Sportblatt*, 'Why is it?' As a matter of fact, there are many causes that go to produce such a state of things regarding the blue variety of Great Danes. First, because the specimens of this colour continue to be exhibited with the blacks, which latter are far better in type. Secondly, judges, as a rule, rather overlook the blue variety. And, thirdly, there exists so few blue Danes that there is not much material for refreshing the blood, which can easily be seen from the stud books of the German Great Dane Club, and also from the fact that the few blue Great Danes that still remain in Germany do not possess the required size, type of head, neck, and substance.

"The question arises, therefore : What is to be done in order to maintain this rare and beautiful colour? German Great Dane fanciers, whose opinion is voiced by the secretary of the German Club, think that the blue Great Danes should be allotted a class for themselves at shows, and I may mention *en passant* that a request to the above effect has already been lodged with the German Great Dane Club ; furthermore, Great Dane judges should be acquainted with the difficulties which are in the way of breeding this colour, and be requested to act accordingly—*i.e.*, to be more lenient when judging the blue variety. However, the most important point is to find fresh blood for the ' blues,' which point is the most difficult, of course, but it can and must be remedied. The story told by the secretary of the German Great Dane Club as to how he started breeding Great Danes with a couple of blue Danes about 10 weeks old may also be considered as the history of the popularity of this variety in Germany, and it should also interest and instruct the amateurs of this colour in England. The secretary bred twice with a litter brother and sister, with the result that although he obtained blue Great Danes they were not quite satisfactory, and the secretary decided to introduce fresh blood, and he therefore placed his blue dog Tyras at walk in the country, so as to be able to use him again when necessary. He then tried to find another blue dog for his bitches, but without effect, and he was obliged, therefore, to use the colour that was most suitable next—*i.e.*, the fawn. Our friend bought a dog of the latter colour which, just as his blue Danes, had no pedigree. One of his blue bitches was consequently mated to the above dog, a very big, beautiful fawn without any markings, with heavy bone, big heavy head, short neck—in a word, absolutely the opposite to the elegant blue bitch. The litter contained five puppies, one dog and two bitches blue, and one dog and one bitch drab-coloured. One of the puppies, a blue bitch, died on the third day, and it is curious to note that in those times in Germany, fanciers, especially ladies, were very keen on drab-coloured Danes (something between blue and fawn). The secretary in question went on hoping that the drab-coloured specimens would turn out blue after all, which, however, was not the case, and he presented the two to a gardener, with the condition that the two animals should always be at his disposal for crossing purposes if necessary. He also gave away to an uncle of his the blue bitch (the mother of the puppies), but kept for himself the young blue couple, which became very typical, and the same can be said of the drab-coloured couple. A curious incident happened here : The two bitches (the blue and the drab) became heavy in whelp at the age of ten months, which the secretary and the gardener could not explain, until the puzzle was solved by the bitches themselves when at the age of between 11 and 12 months : having been served by their brothers during the first heat, they whelped 7 and 6 puppies respectively. This is, however, not so interesting as the fact that the pure blue pair without any markings brought into the world drab-coloured puppies, whereas the drabs of the gardener produced pure blues with small markings on the toes. The youngsters thrived wonderfully well ; they became very strong and big, so that our secretary thought he had at last founded a real breeding strain. However, on account of his private business he was obliged to sell all his Great Danes, with the exception of a dog, which he placed with his parents.

" The aforesaid trial of breeding blue Great Danes confirmed the secretary in his opinion that it is the fawn colour which, better than any other, is capable of improving the breeding of blue Great Danes, and the secretary is against crossing with black specimens if only on account of the fact that the latter, originating as they do from black-and-white harlequins, transmit too much white. Should absolutely pure fawn-bred strains not exist, then only those fawn Danes should be used for breeding blue Danes who have proved themselves capable of transmitting their fawn colour to the progeny. Such fawn

Danes will have for their task to maintain the type and the size, whereas their blue partners will look after the maintaining of the blue colour. The progeny of such a union should be bred from, and the litter brothers and sisters should be crossed with each other again. Of course, in this case the use of not pure-coloured specimens would be unavoidable. The colours that should not be used would be the blue-brindles, using only the blues and those ' miscoloured ' ones that are whole-coloured. However, such a very difficult breeding-course is not to be recommended to those who wish to make a living out of it, and also to those who do not possess the necessary patience ; but it can be recommended to those who wish to contribute towards the *renaissance* of the beautiful blue Great Danes, and to those who would like to make a name for themselves in breeding them, but whose endeavours for the good of the breed have not been sufficiently recognised.

" Every Great Dane breeder, however, should make it a point to keep for breeding purposes the stock obtained from breeding fawns with blues, in order to be able to bring his or her experiments to a successful issue ; but, as it would be well-nigh impossible for one breeder to keep all the stock in his or her kennels, he or she should find a ready market for the surplus, at a low price, with the condition that the stock thus sold should be always held at the seller's disposal whenever he or she wishes to continue the experiment.

G. HOROWITZ."

BREEDING BLUE GREAT DANES.

" I was very interested in Mr. Geo. Horowitz's remarks on breeding blues in his above article on Great Danes. But breeders must remember that in this country the various colours have not been kept so distinctly separate as in Germany. Consequently, I do not consider blue to fawn a good mating, unless a pure fawn strain can be arrived at for the purpose. My own experience shows that too recent brindle ancestry behind fawns mated to blues produces a preponderance of blacks. I believe I have bred more blues than any other British fancier, but, in some twenty blue to fawn matings, only one litter gave a satisfactory proportion of blues. On

CH. SHEBA OF OUBOROUGH.

Photo., A. Dauer, München.

PAMPA OF OUBOROUGH.

the other hand, I found that blue to blue-brindle gave mostly blues.

" Blue to harlequin is certainly inclined to give white markings to the blue puppies, but also produces some good harlequins. Further, most British harlequins have a certain amount of blue breeding behind them, and, as there were no blues in the country after the war, except for my own strain, I have adopted this mating. Blue to black (harlequin bred) is better, but, though I have seen many beautiful black bitches, I have never seen a black dog that appealed to me.

" There is no reason why blues should be any smaller than the other colours. Being darker, they don't look as big as harlequins, fawns, or golden brindles.

" My own opinion is that until fresh blue blood is imported blue to harlequin or black (harlequin bred) is the best mating to adopt. Breeding blue brother to sister is not advisable unless they are already well out-bred, and provided also that a good outcross can be obtained for the next generation. I am of opinion, contrary to Mr. Horowitz, as I think that British blues are now at least equal to the very best of other colours as regards head and neck, and attribute these good points largely to their descent from the imported Prince of ˙Osterstein (blue) and Figaro of St. Austell (harlequin) —(Mrs.) H. M. Cowan "—in " Our Dogs."

CHAPTER IX.

Feeding.

The feeding of dogs is so very important and so connected with breeding that it will be as well to first consider the subject of food apart from the special feeding of Great Danes.

The growth and development of an animal depend in the first place on the character of the food it consumes ; or, to put it very simply, according to the kind of food supplied so the body varies, for the whole animal is built up indirectly from the chemical elements in its food.

Broadly speaking, the best families of our various breeds have been raised to their present state of superiority by continued attention to feeding and breeding, and it cannot be said that either of these agencies has played the more important *role* in amelioration since both are equally necessary to produce and maintain improvement. This being the case, it follows that highly bred young stock require better food than do indifferent animals, and the breeder who gives the best stock the same food and treatment as their inferior brethren will find that they will deteriorate,* for the development of an organism is limited by its environment, and common every-day stock represents the highest standard which can be attained under ordinary every-day management. Improved breeding involves improved feeding, and to say that " it costs no more to keep a good dog than a poor one " is to say what is not true. It costs considerably more to

---

* One of our best-known breeders disagrees with this statement but as he is the only one I could find who holds this view it may be assumed that he is wrong. Curiously enough he owns a dog which is a living example of what I have written. It is a magnificent animal but until he took it in hand and fed it properly it was comparatively worthless.

properly maintain highly bred animals than common ones ; but the profits are proportionately greater. Failure with ordinary breeds is seldom due to ill luck, being generally due to false economy and bad management. Good feeding and good breeding should go together. One is the coefficient of the other, and both have shared in producing our present-day dogs. It is only by the most judicious care in feeding as well as in breeding that the standard of excellence thus reached can be maintained.

It is hardly necessary, I think, in a book of this size, to go into the chemical details ; it will be sufficient if I mention that the constituents of the foods which are of direct use to the animal are the nitrogen compounds, some few mineral matters, which are required for the building up of the body, and the fats and carbohydrates which are the fuel and supply the heat and energy.

Nitrogen enters largely into the composition of the body. It builds up the framework of animals, being the basis of lean flesh (muscular tissue), bones, tendons, brain, nerves, skin, hair and all the working parts and fluids of the body. No new growth can take place without it. The nitrogenous com-pounds occurring in animal and vegetable foods are for the sake of brevity and simplicity designated by the collective term "protein." Thus the protein of a ration is its total content of nitrogenous compounds.

The carbonaceous or fuel nutrients of foods are mainly carbohydrates and fat. They are used in the body to main-tain animal heat and to furnish energy for muscular power, and cannot alone sustain life, as they do not contain protein for building and repairing work.

The nutrients may to some extent do one another's work, the functions of carbohydrates and fat being similar, while protein can be used as fuel ; but no other nutrient under any circumstances can replace protein for building and repairing purposes.

Now, as I have already said, no new growth can take place without nitrogen, so that animals could not live for any long period without it, and nitrogenous (protein supply-ing) foods are absolutely necessary to build up growing stock, to repair the daily waste of tissue in mature dogs, for the production of young, and to supply the nitrogenous matter in milk, blood, digestive juices and other bodily secretions. Thus the proper development of all dogs depends largely on the nitrogen-suppliers constituting a considerable part of the ration. Unfortunately, these foods are usually the most costly, and many dogs suffer from an insufficiency of them. Dogs receiving palatable, varied and digestible rations, containing liberal quantities of protein of animal origin, grow more rapidly, and have stronger, larger bone, and more vigorous organs than those fed mainly on starchy carbonaceous foods so that the rations of breeding stock should be mainly nitrogenous, and consist largely of meat.

Vegetable products like flour, meals, biscuits and rice contain very similar chemical compounds, but in different proportions, and either group will sustain life for a considerable time ; but animal foods in general are the more complete, more concentrated, and more completely digestible.

In the management of all stock it is essential to consider the natural tastes of the animal, which depend to a large extent on their conformation. Herbivorous animals require a large quantity of food, as the nutriment is not concentrated in vegetables, and owing to the fact that they require a considerable bulk of food their digestive systems are proportionately very extensive ; carnivorous animals, on the other hand, which take their food in a concentrated form, have relatively very simple digestive organs.

While admitting that the canine race was originally carnivorous, it cannot be denied that it is now omnivorous ; but the assertion which is made by some people that meat is no longer necessary is manifestly absurd, for the small digestive system of the dog is still essentially that of the carnivorous type of animal, and therefore adapted for the reception of concentrated meat rations rather than for the digestion of more bulky and starchy foods.

Also, the teeth of a dog are essentially those of a carnivorous animal, nor are there any teeth suitable for the crushing and grinding of food such as we find in the horse and ox. The incisors and canines are essentially adapted for tearing flesh while the carnassial or back teeth are formed in scissor-like manner for cutting, but not for grinding.

CH. RUFFLYN REGAN.

LAUREINE OF AXWELL.

The food which we give to our animals cannot be healthful and adequate unless it supplies sufficient nutriment in a form naturally suited for their digestive system. It is only when, in reason, we follow nature's design by largely feeding concentrated meat rations that we can rationally count on our dogs attaining their highest state of physical development. It is obvious that a diet consisting of the animal body and its products must contain all the constituents required for the growth and maintenance of another animal body and its products.

The intelligence and "life"—or spirit—of a dog largely depend on its getting the nourishment it was constructed to assimilate and we cannot expect that a dog fed mainly on farinaceous foods will exhibit the greatest courage and endurance—the spirit which we desire—or the highest degree of intelligence. Meat and bones appease a dog's hunger better than vegetable foods, and they produce firm muscle and growth of frame, while farinaceous foods increase the deposition of fat. Dogs fed mainly or entirely on farinaceous foods may put on flesh, but their systems become weakened and predisposed to disease. Vegetable foods excite the vital functions less than animal foods, the contrast in activity and muscular vigour between carnivorous and herbivorous animals being generally very marked, while the muscle of carnivorous animals contracts very much more rapidly than does that of herbivorous or omnivorous animals. Another very interesting point worked out by Mr. Cornish Bowden relates to the breeding powers of dogs fed on vegetarian diet. Mr. Cornish Bowden finds that a dog so fed will have a very small family, and that any attempt to breed from the family will be a failure, however the other mating dog may be fed. In other words, the offspring of a vegetarian-fed dog are all sterile. Claud Bernard and Magendie have shown that dogs can be kept alive for an indefinite time on meat alone, but not so on starchy foods. Fresh vegetables should not be considered* as dog foods, and if used at all should be given very sparingly.

It is generally believed that dogs require a certain amount of hard food to keep their teeth clean and to stimulate the

* When used with meat and biscuits, I think vegetables are of great help ; it is when used as a " food " alone that I consider them of little or no value.

flow of saliva, and that if beef or mutton bones are not given they should be allowed a certain number of hard biscuits. I do not think in reality that any of the bone eaten reaches the junction of tooth and gum where the tartar collects. It is quite right to keep the teeth clean, but I think that a tooth-brush and carbolic tooth powder is much more efficient as a dentifrice than bones or biscuits.

The dog foods may be divided into those of (*a*) Animal origin and (*b*) Vegetable origin. Taking the former first, we find under this heading :—

MEAT.—The instinctive desire which a normal dog has for meat is a sure sign that it is really required for nutritive pur-poses, and is that which is best suited for its digestive system ; whilst its indifference to some other food materials is as sure evidence of their less worth for nourishment and unsuitability.

Sound, good horse-meat is in all respects as valuable a food for dogs as beef, but care must be taken to avoid diseased meat by only dealing with a slaughterer whom one can depend on, and who realises what the meat is wanted for. Meat that is of pale pink colour, unusually wet, soft, or flabby, or has a disagreeable cadaverous smell, especially when cut up and rinsed with warm water, is unwholesome. Good meat should have no smell, be firm and elastic to the touch, barely moisten the fingers, and be dry on the surface.

The fact that many dogs eat putrid meat without apparent injury is evidence that the effect of habit confers considerable immunity, but not that putrid meat is desirable. Meat is at times measly or infested with encysted parasites, some-times visible to the naked eye as small yellowish spots. Thoroughly cooking the meat destroys all these parasites, and does away with all dangers. Tripe and sheep's paunch, though not so nitrogenous as mutton or beef, are, when thoroughly cleaned and boiled, very easily digested, and are excellent food for puppies. Liver, which dogs are very fond of, is by reason of its richness rather an irritant, but blood is of great value, and second only to flesh itself. When fresh and well-cooked it makes splendid food, and it has the great advantage that it is easily obtained in towns.

BONES consist chiefly of mineral matter and ash. They contain little or no nutriment, and although the majority of our domesticated dogs enjoy them, their value as a food is probably greatly discounted by the amount of harm that is caused by them. I certainly advocate giving puppies and young dogs bones they cannot eat, to " cut " their teeth on and harden the gums ; they also promote the flow of saliva and strengthen the jaws. On the other hand, they are a frequent cause of tooth trouble ; they not only wear the teeth unduly, but often cause dental trouble by bruising the alveolar and peridental membranes, causing abscesses, and often ruining the teeth. They cause constipation by reason of the excess of lime salts they contain ; and also when swallowed in large pieces they often pass into the intestines undigested, in this way causing a blocking of the bowel very hard to dislodge. I might add that if given too often they cause excessive development of the masseter muscle, and spoil the dog's head, making it " cheeky." Game and poultry bones of all sorts should always be avoided, as there is a tendency in them, when crushed or broken by the jaws, to sliver, and many a good dog has met its end by such pieces perforating and cutting the stomach and intestines.

GREAVES or graves is the residue left when refuse meat, etc., is boiled down to extract the valuable fat for commercial purposes. The residue is pressed into cakes, and eventually broken up and mixed with broken biscuits to be sold as houndmeal. The experience of most unprejudiced users is that dogs fed much on greaves are liable to sudden attacks of diarrhœa. When other animal food is unobtainable, greaves is better than nothing ; but it is wise to buy direct from the maker, and only such a quantity as can be used while still quite fresh.

MILK is often described as a perfect food, for it contains all the necessary elements of food. It unquestionably is a perfect food for the young of the animal producing the milk, but not necessarily so for that of other animals. A cow's milk is not perfect food for a puppy, as a bitch's milk is about three times as rich as a cow's. Milk is not a perfect food theoretically for mature dogs or older puppies ; but practically it seems to serve as an admirable sole food for the latter, as will be seen when mention is made of Sir Claud Alexander's method of rearing his stock, both wild and domesticated.*

Skim milk and buttermilk are useful adjuncts to other food, but they do not of course contain so much fat as ordinary milk. Condensed milk is not advisable, in spite of the fact that puppies apparently thrive on it for a time. CREAM is really milk with a greater proportion of fat. On account of its expense few people give it ; but I do not think they would hesitate to use butter, which is practically of a uniform composition if they only realised that it is just as useful as cream, if emulsified in milk.

MILK POWDERS, DRIED MILK.—These powders really consist of milk, the liquid portion of which has been evaporated and the residue ground into a fine powder after all the moisture has been drawn off by intense heat. The powder produced contains all the solid nutrients of milk, and by being dissolved in hot water can be made to closely resemble boiled milk. The powders are made in three qualities—(1) Whole cream milk powder made from whole milk ; (2) Half cream milk powder made from milk from which half the cream has been taken ; and (3) Skim milk powder, which contains no cream. The full cream milk powder, as already mentioned, is most valuable in feeding puppies, the proper proportion being 2½oz. of full cream powder to half a pint of fresh cow's milk. Full cream milk powder is approximately eight times as concentrated as fresh cow's milk.†

EGGS are a nutritive food slightly more concentrated than bitches' milk, and of the greatest value for weak puppies or older dogs that are ill.

FISH is not as nourishing, satisfying or stimulating as flesh meat.‡ It requires to be eaten in larger quantities, and is really only of value in that it makes a variety in the diet.

COD LIVER OIL is a food fat obtained from the liver of different fishes. It is easily borne by the stomach, and

* See page 100, et seq.
† As some fanciers to whom I have recommended the milk powders have found some difficulty in procuring it, I may say that it can always be obtained from Mr. Prideaux, Dairyman, Motcombe, Shaftesbury, Dorset ; but any good dairyman ought to be able to make it.
‡ Mackerel is an exception to this, as it contains 23·5 per cent. proteid to the 22 per cent. of beef. *Theory and Practice of Hygiene.* Notter & Firth. pp. 280-297.

88

hence peculiarly suitable for weakly, ricketty puppies and aged dogs. Teaspoonful doses are quite large enough to begin with, it should never be given in large quantities, and only after or with food, for otherwise it only irritates the stomach. Though really a medicine, it is so constantly used when there is any weakness that it is more convenient to mention it among the foodstuffs.

Foods of Vegetable Origin.

Rice contains a large proportion of starch, and very little nitrogenous, fatty and mineral matter. Associated with meat, it constitutes a valuable dog food, being easily digestible and having no laxative action.

Wheat Flour is a useful food, usually given in the form of biscuits, bread, and puddings. Stale bread is easily digestible, but new bread is much less so. Bread baked to a biscuit colour is generally much appreciated. Bread and flour, if kept in a moist place, are likely to become sour and acid and even biscuits, if stored for long, are subject to injury by various insects classed popularly as weevils. Apart from loss of weight such pests deteriorate the alimentary value of the stored food. It is the poorest economy to give inferior or damaged food because it appears cheap. A good dog deserves the best of food, and it pays to provide it.

Suet and macaroni are often relished in illness when other foods are rejected.

Oatmeal is rich in nitrogenous food, but it requires very thorough cooking. It is rather too laxative, irritating and heating for dogs, but may be used as a change.

Cornmeal or Maize Meal is richer in fat and contains less protein than wheat flour. It is a fattening food and should not be kept for long.

Barley Meal holds an average position as a dog food, but is not often used, especially for dogs with an impaired digestion, as it is less palatable and less digestible than wheaten flour.

Potatoes are three-quarters composed of water and the rest is mainly starch, so that in spite of their popularity with many people they are a bulky and innutritious food, very prone to cause eczema.

FRESH VEGETABLES are not dog foods, though many eat and some relish them. Occasionally used, they act as an alterative and mild laxative for overfed and under exercised dogs, but if used generally they cause an immense amount of disease and suffering. As already pointed out, the dog's stomach is small and adapted only to receiving small quantities of food in a concentrated form. If the stomach is filled with fresh vegetables, which are bulky and comparatively not nutritious, the result is inevitably indigestion and malnutrition. Even if vegetables were a food naturally suited to the canine digestive system—which they are not—a dog could not obtain from them nutrients they do not contain.

Chemical analysis will not teach everything, for it is not so much the chemical composition of a ration that counts as the amount of nourishment the dog gets out of the food. A food substance which cannot be digested by a particular species of animal is obviously undesirable as food for that species, no matter how high its chemical nutrients or how great its worth for feeding other kinds of domesticated stock.

WATER, which constitutes about half the weight of living dogs, is essential for them, as it both carries nutriment into the body and is the means of removing waste products. It should therefore be a rule to allow dogs all the fresh pure water which they desire, and there should always be a plentiful supply in an accessible place. The actual quantity of water required appears to depend greatly upon the individuality of the dog, for I have known a dog in the best of health drink quite five times as much water as any of its kennel mates.

So much then for the different foods, and we arrive at the important question as to feeding with raw or cooked meat.

Cooking has the effect of developing flavour, exciting appetite and destroying parasites, but certain important constituents boil out in the process, and are lost unless the liquor is fed with the meat. The most convenient plan is to remove the cooked meat and thoroughly boil rice or various meals in the liquor. The meat can be fed after the pudding so obtained, or may be chopped up and added to it. For those who prefer to make their pudding with water it is advisable to plunge the meat into boiling water before cooking, as by so doing a coating of coagulated albumen is formed, which causes the retention of "the goodness of the meat." Broth can, of course, always be reduced in volume and increased in richness by boiling down, but however long the meat is boiled it still contains some of the mineral salts and nearly all the protein it originally contained.

In many vegetable foods (cereals) the starch is contained in tiny thick walled cells, on which the digestive fluids have but little effect. Cooking ruptures these and makes the starch more soluble. Some foods require very prolonged cooking, oatmeal, for instance, wanting at least three hours boiling before it is fit food for a dog. It is very inadvisable to let dogs have anything to eat which is much above the temperature of the body, as, if too hot, it cracks the enamel and tends to early decay of the teeth. Palatability or relish of food is of considerable importance, as though appetising odours and flavours do not furnish nutriment they probably help to a complete assimilation of the food taken. Animals do not do so well on a food which they do not like, even if it is highly nutritious, and it is commonly accepted that a dog generally thrives better on a fairly well balanced ration that is eaten with avidity, than on one more perfectly constituted but less relished.

While it is most desirable to prepare dogs' foods in a tempting manner, it must be strongly impressed on everyone that condimental flavourings are altogether wrong. Highly seasoned foods, and some of those on the market are extremely so, do an immense amount of harm in spoiling dogs' appetites, and often produce diarrhœa and skin disease. While different foodstuffs vary widely in their nutritive value, and so are not of equal value as dog foods, it is found that some variety is essential to the best health and development. A mixed ration, consisting largely of various meats with reasonable additions of farinaceous foods, is the most sensible diet for ordinary dogs, because variety increases palatability, and so stimulates appetite and digestion and promotes health.

A food that is appetising and wholesome for one dog may be distasteful to, or may actually disagree, with another, and in a large kennel it will be found that a successful and observant kennel man will feed some of his dogs quite differently from the rest.

The number of times a day a dog should be fed is a matter of considerable difference of opinion among fanciers, though most authorities advise one full meal a day for an adult dog. They probably do so because carnivorous animals thrive best if fed at long intervals. The dog, however, is an omnivorous animal, and from personal experience and from the best physiological evidence, I am sure that a fairly big meal at night and a light one in the morning, with a couple of hard biscuits to keep him occupied during the day, is the best way of feeding. Moderate quantities of food at reasonable intervals are more easily and completely digested than are larger quantities at long intervals. The evening is the best time for the large meal, except with dogs required for protective purposes, as they go to sleep contentedly with a full stomach, have nothing to occupy them except digestion, and thus do not annoy people by barking at night. Adult dogs should not have more than two meals, as too frequent feeding, instead of providing extra nourishment, sets up digestive disorders and results in less nutrients being digested and assimilated.

Dogs should on no account be fed immediately before or after hard exercise, and will indeed seldom eat when tired out, while, if they do, the food is not properly digested as the stomach is not in a fit state to receive it.

Many dog owners consider that regularity in feeding times is of no practical importance, arguing from the case of the butcher's dog who gets his food at odd hours, but is generally in good condition. The butcher's dog, however, lives mainly upon a combination of various meats, and its usual state of fitness is probably largely due to this rather than to its being fed at irregular intervals. Regularity in feeding tends to produce a regular habit of appetite. Sudden changes in the quantity or character of the food supplied should be avoided, an abrupt change from an accustomed food to one widely dissimilar often producing diarrhœa or some other digestive disturbance.

PRIMLEY NINA.

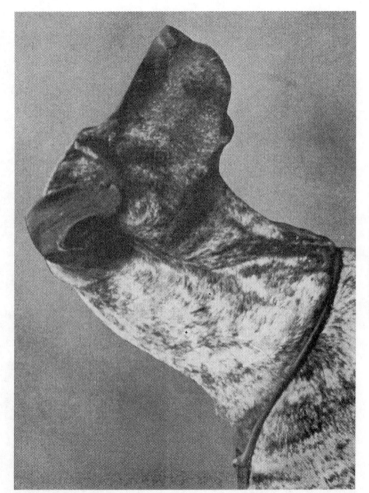

PRIMLEY NINA (Head Study).

A reasonable degree of uniformity as regards the quantity of food supplied must also be observed, while the amount of food a dog will eat must not be confounded with the amount that he can profitably use. Perfect development depends on the quantity of nutrients well digested and assimilated, not upon the largeness of the amount of food actually eaten. Personal idiosyncrasy must also be considered, one dog eating nearly twice as much as another that is his physical counterpart. It is quite impossible to lay down a law as to how much food should be given to any dog. One can only be guided by observation. A good appetite is almost as essential as is good food to satisfy it, and in consequence dogs must never be surfeited. An empty plate suggests sufficiency as well as scarcity ; and the fact that there is nothing left after a meal does not necessarily mean that a dog has not had enough. Indeed, the secret of successful feeding is never to allow a healthy animal a chance of leaving any food. Loss of appetite is usually due to (1) overfeeding, (2) giving damaged, fermented or filthy food, (3) one kind of food too long without change, (4) too starchy ration, or (5) sore mouth. No detailed advice can be given, and each owner must find out the cause for himself. The quantity of nourishment required to keep a dog in good condition increases with the amount of exercise and degree of cold which it undergoes, inactivity and warmth lessening the amount. In early life one has to consider the function of growth, and with a brood bitch the nourishment of her puppies. Weight for weight the growing dog needs more food than the adult.

Apart from containing adequate nutrients, foods must have a certain bulk to properly distend the digestive organs, and so enable the gastric juice to act to its greatest advantage. Bulky foods usually contain a lot of water or are innutritious, and there is a danger of dogs being inadvertently overfed ; this may be minimised by feeding with naturally concentrated meat foods, a reasonable proportion of bulky foodstuffs, and so keeping the dog satisfied without risking indigestion.

It is not sufficient to give dogs food that they will eat. The nutritive value of a food depends on the proportion of its nutrients which are digested and utilised rather than upon the total content of nutrient substance. Mere ease of digestion is a much less vital attribute of foods for ordinarily healthy dogs than is the completeness with which the nutrients of a food can be used up. The digestibility of a food depends largely on the natural tastes of the species of animal to be fed, and it has been found from careful study that the highest degree of digestibility of a nutrient is usually found in foods containing the largest amounts of that nutrient.

Over-feeding is one of the commonest causes of illness in dogs, for food eaten in excess of that needed for the efficient nourishment of the body overtaxes the digestive system just as the use of unsuitable food does, and is quite as harmful. The effect of over-indulgence in food may be very serious, for overfat animals do not breed readily, do not endure parturition well or work properly, and are specially susceptible to disease. Too much food may be worse than too little, and have a directly opposite result to what is intended, as over-feeding impairs the digestion more quickly than under-feeding. The breeder's aim should be to keep his stock neither fat nor thin, but to allow every dog, whatsoever its habit and age, enough nourishing food to maintain it in thrifty, profitable condition, so that puppies attain their maximum development and the brood bitch and stud dog remain in good flesh.

Under-feeding may result not only from insufficient bulk of food but also from the use of too innutritious or indigestible food materials. Thus many dogs, living solely or mainly on farinaceous foods, may be underfed though receiving large rations—may be starving with stomachs full. Insufficient or defective food is harmful and expensive at all times, but especially so during the growing and gestative periods. Young growth is cheap growth, and as an instance I may refer to our own breed ; it costs at least twice as much to add an inch in height to a Great Dane at the age of six months as it would have done at half that age. Imperfect nutrition not only arrests present growth but seems to lessen the capacity for future development as well, so that its effects persist to some degree through life. Many breeders, who recognise the importance of supplying plenty of nourishing food to puppies and bitches in whelp or suckling young, are not equally solicitous about their other stock, though a deficient diet is, in the long run, much more costly than rational liberal feeding, for ill-nourished animals can never make the full return they would naturally be capable of under more favourable conditions. If, from a perverted view of economy, we reduce the vigour of our breeding stock, not only do the profits disappear, but the cost of maintenance remains to be borne out of pocket ; and cumulative experience clearly shows us that the only certain method of avoiding this risk is to supply breeding dogs with an ample sufficiency of good food all the year round. To be as profitable as possible, dogs must be well cared for at all times. If they do not pay to feed, they will certainly not do so to starve. Good food is as essential as good blood, and the breeding of high - class stock never yet paid where liberal nourishment and care were not provided.

The subjects of food and health are very closely related, for the vigorous condition resulting from nourishment is, perhaps, the best safeguard against disease. Indeed, by sensible and generous feeding, it is often possible to so tone up the system as to overcome, or hold in latent condition, morbid hereditary predispositions, while, on the other hand, constitutions with a slight natural tendency to weakness are so debilitated by injudicious or scanty feeding as to become specially susceptible to disease. As I have mentioned before, it is one of the gravest of hygienic mistakes to feed dogs almost exclusively on biscuits, bread, and patent starchy foods, and other grave errors I have dealt with are overfeeding and unsuitable feeding at wrong intervals. Medicine is only a temporary expedient when dogs are improperly fed, and when well fed and well managed they seldom need any physic at all. The successful breeder does not wait to cure, he is quick to prevent, for it is infinitely better to stave off disease by carefully studying the daily wants and needs of our dogs than to cure it when it has appeared. If only as a matter of business it is cheaper to provide good food and care in advance.

The successful treatment of sick animals depends largely upon their proper feeding. It is generally essential to maintain the patient's strength while the illness runs its course and nature effects a cure, but, unfortunately, the appetite during sickness is often very capricious; if so, the food must be made as appetising and varied as possible, consistent with suitability. If a dish is refused it should be removed at once and offered later. When recovery is dependent on the strength being kept up, dogs which refuse food must be forced to eat small quantities at regular intervals, but this plan should not be adopted until every legitimate means of tempting a failing appetite has been used.* Dogs will often eat raw eggs or scraped meat when they refuse all else, and a moderate amount of raw meat is a great factor for good in almost all diseases (except canine distemper†) if it can only be kept down, for it is the most easily digested, wholesome, satisfying and strengthening of foods.

Liquid foods are frequently desirable in diseases of the digestive tract and during fevers. Eggs beaten up and beef juice pressed out of raw meat are two of the most useful foods in bad cases, while milk and the full cream milk powder form invaluable adjuncts to these. Many of the meat extracts are useless as nourishment, containing only the flavouring matter, while beef tea, as ordinarily prepared, is a stimulant rather than food. Beef tea is quite easy to prepare if the proper method is adopted. One pound of meat (or whatever quantity is desired) should be taken, very finely minced, placed in a jar and a pint of cold water added for every one pound of meat used. It should stand in a cool place for four hours, and after this it should be allowed to simmer slowly in an oven for another four hours. By this means, most of the organic salts, soluble albumen and flavouring matters will be dissolved out and the greater part of the nutriment of the meat will be extracted. During this period it should be constantly skimmed to remove the fat. Finally the residue of the cooked minced meat may be pounded, passed through a sieve and added to the liquor. I consider this the only proper way to extract the utmost nutrient value from the meat though it can of course be varied in details.

Stimulants given in measured doses, like other medicines, are of great value in the prostration of acute diseases. It is

* It is better to predigest all foods that have to be given by force.
† In holding this view I am, I know, going against the opinion of many veterinary surgeons, but experience has taught me that, while meat juice may do good in distemper, meat itself is a poison. This is only what we should expect from comparison with human beings and the food they receive in illness. No doctor would think of giving a meat diet to a patient suffering from an acute febrile disease.

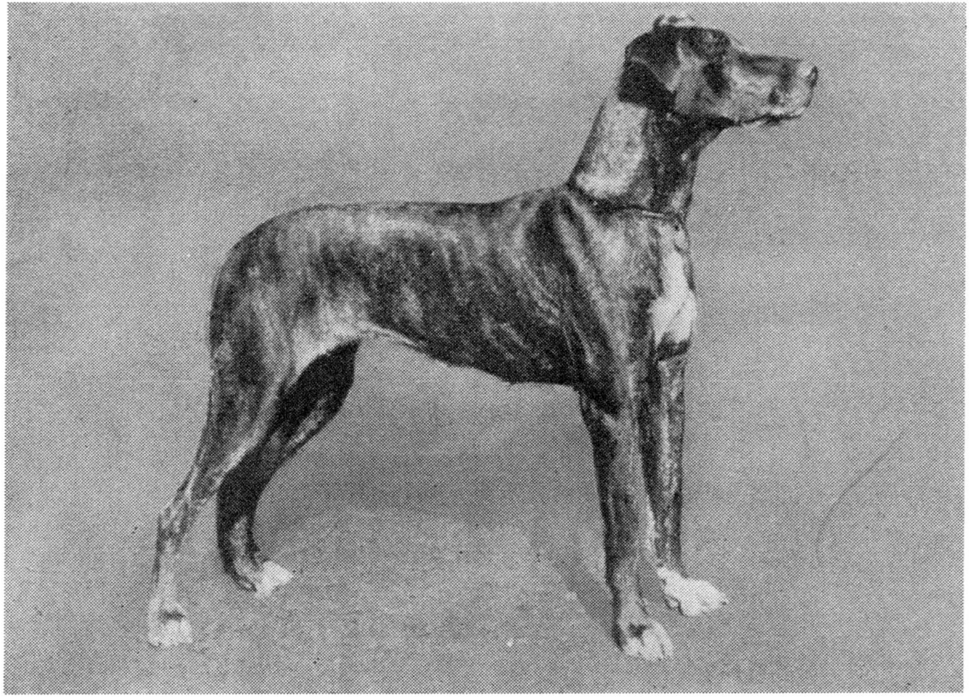

PRIMLEY NEREDA.

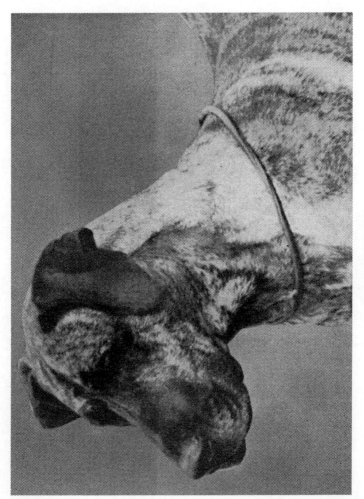

PRIMLEY PAVLOVA.

important in such cases that the patient's strength be maintained until the critical stage is passed, for death often occurs from exhaustion. Alcohol, properly administered, spurs the flagging energies and stimulates the digestive system as well as the heart, so that to get the greatest benefit from its use it should be given with food. Pure brandy is the best alcoholic stimulant for dogs, but good whiskey is better than inferior brandy.

It now only remains for me to mention the feeding of the Great Dane from a somewhat more practical point of view.

THE FEEDING OF THE PUPPIES.

In the young of all species of animals the formation of bone and tissue proceeds very rapidly, and puppies therefore require an abundance of the nutrients needed for building up bone and muscle. Puppies fed on suitable nitrogenous foods grow very strongly and quickly, though their ultimate development is, of course, largely controlled by the more or less fixed constitutional habit of their breed. On the other hand, an excessive amount of starchy food tends to the production of a poor bony framework and muscular system in all young animals. Unfortunately, many people think that any food will do for dogs, and fear that liberal food and good care will make their young stock "tender." As a matter of fact, a well-nourished puppy will generally pass safely through exposure and illness which would carry off a scantily fed one. An immense number of well-bred puppies die when quite young, and though it is often attributed to some incomprehensible degeneration, it is solely because they are improperly fed. Important as are proper kennelling and hygienic conditions, they are, as contrasted with good feeding, unimportant in puppyhood.

The proper feeding of puppies is at first effected by properly feeding their dam, and it must needs be commenced before their birth. She should be well fed and supplied with some powdered calcium phosphate to help to build up the puppies' bones, one teaspoonful daily spread over her meals.

For the first three weeks after they are born the puppies require nothing but their mother's milk. When they can see properly, which is generally in the third week, I begin

I

to teach the pups to lap, and I always use the mixture previously mentioned of full cream milk powder and milk.* This is done not only for their mothers but their own sakes as well. Puppies getting their dams milk supplemented with other suitable foods make a much better and stronger start than those weaned at five or six weeks, no matter how much food and care the latter enjoy. During the fourth and fifth week I add a very little stale crumbled bread to the mixture, or a little well boiled rice, and also give them very small quantities of scraped beef daily. These meals I increase gradually until the puppies are weaned after the sixth week. I consider it most important to start feeding the puppies with meat and bread while they are having their mother's help, as by this method there is no sudden and violent change in the feeding, and the pups have their dam's milk to rely on as well as that which is given them. Our object should be, while avoiding sudden changes, to feed such suitable foods as, in view of their age, the puppies can reasonably be expected to digest without discomfort. On the vigour and strength acquired during puppyhood the value of a dog at maturity largely depends. Sloppy, watery foods are ordinarily most unwholesome for puppies old enough to digest concentrated rations. Such foods do not furnish sufficient nutrients for their bulk ; they unduly distend the stomach and conduce to indigestion and scouring. When the puppies are completely weaned the character of their meals is at first exactly the same, but instead of being fed three or four times, as they were when with their mother, they now require to be fed every 2 hours, with an occasional stretch of 3 hours, between seven o'clock in the morning and nine or ten at night. I give, as an example, a diet table used by a well known and successful fancier : 7 a.m., milk ; 9 a.m., boiled rice, milk, and egg ; 12 mid-day, meat ; 2 p.m., bread and milk ; 4 p.m., rice and milk ; 6 p.m., milk ; 8 p.m., meat ; 10 p.m., milk. A little phosphate of calcium should be added to one of the rice and milk meals.

The puppies' stomachs are not constructed to stow away large quantities of food at a time, so that to furnish them with all they have capacity for, involves supplying small amounts at short intervals. Giving suitable foods regularly—a little

* See page 88.

at a time and often—sums up the whole art of puppy feeding; and good feeding, warmth, and cleanliness are the principal secrets of rearing puppies. By three months, the number of meals will be reduced to five, now all solid or semi-solid meals (including two of meat) and a good bone to gnaw, and so the number is gradually reduced to three and finally to two. It is not necessary to specify the exact food to be given, nor would it be possible, as what suits one dog will not suit another. I always give one meal entirely, or very nearly entirely, made of meat (in the first year often two) while the other meals are made of dry bread, rice, and various meals or biscuits made into a pudding with the broth from the cooked meat. The greater part of the meat I use is horse flesh, and while a considerable quantity is given raw I always cook enough to get sufficient broth for a pudding. I do not think there is anything more to be said about the dog's food from its puppyhood to adult age, except so far as a bitch in whelp or a stud dog is concerned; I might, however, mention that nearly all the biscuits in the market are very good if not used for too long at a time. Variety is a most important thing, and I never think of using any of the special biscuits for longer than a week at a time, excellent though they are.

Although the food and the method of feeding which I have mentioned is with some slight variations that which is generally adopted it is only right that I should describe as fully as possible a very different plan which is followed by a dog fancier and a naturalist of very great experience and which in his hands has certainly proved more successful than the method commonly adopted, in that his young stock have been free since its inception from the many ailments that attack puppies and also the young of the Felidæ, which are more delicate than the Canidæ. Sir Claud Alexander has been an exhibitor of dogs for well over thirty years and, as he also keeps a very large collection of wild animals besides being a most successful exhibitor of cats, his remarks and experience demand the greatest respect and cannot fail to make every thoughtful fancier wonder whether the method of rearing young animals that is commonly followed is the right one. This is particularly brought home when we read what is said about infantile ailments. My knowledge of Sir Claud's method came from a conversation which we had at the Kennel Club, and I do not think that I can do better than give the letter which he sent me in its entirety, as it gives, most concisely, the various steps followed in the feeding of a litter. Sir Claud writes :—

" Dear Dr. Mackenzie,

" I hardly know how to write the letter you ask for ; the subject is too large for a letter, and ought to be treated in a series of articles (the management of dogs and other carnivora in captivity, treatment of distemper by starvation, etc.). I have had such a series in my mind for some time, but, until an editor appears just when I have time to write, it will remain a thing of the future. I will, however, put down very shortly our way of feeding puppies, and leave you to quote anything you think worth noting.

" (1) Bitches in pup are fed, as at other times, once a day, until the pups are three weeks old, when the food is increased, or even doubled—but they are still fed only once, in the mornings.

" (2) At about three weeks, the dam is gradually taken away in the daytime, till at four and a half weeks she is only with the pups at night.

" (3) From four weeks the pups have as much warm milk as they will drink greedily once a day—as soon as they drink well they get it twice.

" (4) At about eight weeks the pups are entirely weaned, but still have nothing except milk twice a day, until a relaxed condition of the bowels or the appearance of a permanent tooth suggests a change. Then a few bits of bread are floated in the milk, and a *very* small feed of *dry cooked* meat cut up very small (from one to two ounces for a pup of average size—a wolf or a collie) is given at mid-day.

" (5) This small amount of meat is gradually increased to about four ounces, and when the pup is half through his teething, one milk ration is taken off and he has two meals per day—one of milk and the other of dry cooked meat to which a little *dry* bread is added (say two or three ounces). This goes on till the permanent teeth are all through, when

100

RUBY OF EVERLEY.

PRINCE OF EVERLEY.

" (6) The puppy goes on to the ration of the adults—raw meat with the addition of as much bread or bone as may be required to regulate the bowels.

" You will notice that I have said nothing about rickets, your original subject, for the simple reason that since we have adopted this system, we have not had a single ricketty, wormy, or pot-bellied puppy or kitten.

" I have not mentioned exercise either, for beyond their permanent quarters our young stock get practically none. We keep them entirely on wood floors or on dry earth, and if compelled to use stone, brick, or cement floors, we bed them down three or four inches deep in sawdust or moss litter.

" I do not pretend that young carnivora cannot be reared under other conditions, but that this is the only way in which numbers can be reared in close confinement, on the same ground year after year, without loss, I am sure.

" You ask how we arrived at our method, but I cannot tell you. We learned it by degrees, principally from the Felidæ, which are far more delicate and difficult to keep than the Canidæ.

" You also inquire about the constitutions of our young stock, and I can honestly say that they are much better than those of animals whose digestion has been ruined by excessive or improper feeding.

" As an instance of the very small quantity of meat required by immature carnivora, we have just found that ten ounces of meat will cause partial paralysis in leopard cubs seven months old, six ounces being their proper ration. I do not expect to be believed any more than was Cassandra of old, but we are not quite beginners, for I began showing dogs over thirty years ago, and we now have about forty dogs, sixty-five cats, and 100 wild carnivora, all of which are fed entirely by Lady Alexander and myself. No food is used except horse flesh, rib bones, rabbit, and dry bread, and no medicine except castor oil. We never employ a veterinary surgeon except in cases of accident. If you would like to see for yourself I should be very pleased to show you everything if you will run down some day—we are about an hour from Town.   Yours very truly,

CLAUD ALEXANDER."

As I have no personal experience of Sir Claud's method I can express no opinion about it beyond saying that in his hands it has most certainly been extremely successful. I intend to try it at the first opportunity, as it undoubtedly saves a lot of trouble, and must obviously be a great deal cheaper. The most important point in Sir Claud's experience is, at all events to me, the immunity he has had from distemper and the other serious ailments of puppyhood.

FEEDING THE BITCH IN WHELP.

The feeding of the bitch from the time of conception should be such as to best fit her for the strain of bearing and suckling her offspring. It must be remembered that she has to eat for herself and her puppies, and that her food must accordingly be plentiful and good enough to keep her own bodily machine in proper working order, to build up her young and to sustain a generous flow of milk for their nourishment. The object of feeding is not to fatten but to strengthen her, and to furnish ample material for the rapid manufacture of bone and muscular flesh in the puppies. There are owners who deliberately keep brood bitches thin, under the impression that it improves their breeding and suckling qualities. This absurd belief is based on the observation that good milch animals are generally on the thin side, but they are thin because they are good milkers, not good milkers because they are thin. Their leanness is due to the fact that most of their food goes to provide the material and energy needed for abundant milk secretion.

Cold watery foods—never healthful to dogs—are distinctly harmful to the pregnant bitch ; and any food that actively affects the bowels either way should ordinarily be avoided at this time.

Provided a bitch is in reasonable flesh it is not wise to do much for her just before whelping, but if the milk supply is scanty, strong broths and watery fluids will increase its flow. It is not wise, however, to give much immediately after whelping, or the flow of milk may become greater than the puppies can take. When she has been well fed, it is better, in reason, to stint her as to quantity before whelping ; it is at all events preferable to overfeeding. Under normal conditions, ordinary food may be safely given two or three days after whelping, the aim at first being to give only just enough suitable and nourishing food to avoid any risk of the dam's stomach being deranged.

As the puppies grow, better feeding is, of course, required for the mother, as the drain upon her is very heavy. How immense the drain is becomes apparent when one considers the amazing way the puppies grow. This enormous growth comes from the food taken by the mother and converted into milk, which again is secreted from the blood. The blood is derived either from the food, or from the flesh and fat stored in the body, both of which are formed from the food. In view of these facts it is obvious that the bitch requires the best food, nor is it to be wondered that she rapidly loses flesh after the third week however much food may be given to her. The true method of preventing an excessive strain on the bitch is to start feeding her puppies early, and so lessening their demands on her. No matter how much the trouble involved, the puppies must be taught to lap during the third week. Excessive fatty development is as bad a fault as underfeeding, but it is highly injurious to suddenly stop the food supply because the bitch is getting too fat. It is far better to feed a bitch consistently on the muscle and bone-making nutrients rather than on starchy foods, and to give her plenty of exercise right from the start, thus preventing her getting too fat at any time.

I have already mentioned that cases of bitches eating their puppies undoubtedly occur, though I have been fortunate enough to have no personal experience of it. I think, there is no doubt, that improper feeding is generally the origin of this vice, and I do not believe there is any risk of an ordinary bitch developing this trait if she is rationally fed.

FEEDING THE STUD DOG.

At no period of life should the stud dog be stinted, especially when young ; he should always have enough to keep him fit but not fat, for fatness lowers his stud value, and it is difficult to reduce him in flesh without lowering his vitality.

Finally, I would say that the results obtained from any system of feeding depend largely upon the shelter and care which animals receive. A dog deprived of fresh air, sunlight exercise, clean and comfortable kennelling, dry bedding, and other essentials to robust health, cannot make the best use of, or return for, the food it consumes, so that all these matters must be looked to. There are few kennels where they cannot be secured at merely nominal cost ; and cheerful, wholesome life conditions mean cheerful, thrifty, profitable dogs.

The growth and development of an animal depend in the first place on the character of the food it consumes, and I cannot do better that supplement the splendid advice of the late Dr. Mackenzie by reproducing an article which appeared in " Our Dogs " some time ago by that well known authority, Mrs. H. M. Cowan, which will probably be read with much interest by all those who are starting a kennel. This excellent article also gives some very good advice on the important question of exercise. It is as follows :—

" Below I give the procedure adopted in my own kennels. I have included exercise, as the best feeding is wasted without proper exercise.

All grown dogs and bitches get their fill of kibbled biscuits, soaked in broth and with about ½lb. chopped meat (raw or cooked) added, once a day in the evening. Bullock's head, well boiled, is economical, and very nutritious in this connection. It is better than horse flesh, which makes the dogs smell strong. A large mincer or sausage-machine is useful for chopping the meat up.

Bitches should be in hard, muscular condition when mated —not thin, and, above all, not soft and fat. After mating the meat diet above is gradually increased up to 1lb. a day at four weeks, which is usually not exceeded unless the bitch is in poor condition—in which case an extra 1lb. is advisable. A dessert-spoonful of best white fish meal (not the dark, salt, and oily kind) is added throughout pregnancy. This contains vitamines and helps towards the growth of the unborn puppies and their subsequent freedom from rickets. I have a theory (I give it for what it is worth) that limewater, given to a pregnant bitch, stiffens the bones and may cause difficulty in whelping.

After four weeks of pregnancy, a morning feed of biscuits and broth is usually added, but the meat ration is not further increased. During the last few days before whelping, the food is given more sloppy (*i.e.*, more broth is added to the biscuit) and, provided the bitch does not show any excessive secretion of milk, a pint or so of milk a day is added to her feed.

I do not think a bitch can be over-exercised (provided the pace is not excessive) during the first six weeks of pregnancy. Mine usually go out for 8-12 miles a day with the horses or following a bicycle (ridden at a moderate pace). During the last three weeks the exercise is gradually shortened, till at the very end the bitch goes out for only two half-mile walks a day. Jumping should be avoided and the bitch never forced to exert herself unwillingly. But many of my bitches insist on exercising " on their own " by galloping about the fields right up to the end, nor have they ever been the worse for this.

It is a hard and fast rule in my kennels that every bitch is dosed for worms three weeks after mating, and I find I have very little cause to complain of worms in my litters. When the bitch has whelped the majority of her pups, I give her a half-pint of warm milk, which I consider very helpful to her. After whelping, she has nothing but milk, boiled oatmeal, and pearl barley (all given warm) for the first 48 hours—about four bowls a day—(*i.e.*, as much as she will take), with an ounce of limewater in each feed.

On the third day, if the bitch is feeding well and there appears to be no womb trouble, a breakfast-cupful of soaked Osoko is added to each feed. But if a bitch appears the least disinclined to take her food, the Osoko is at once discontinued, as this points to womb trouble, and competent veterinary assistance should be at once called in.

I consider this a most important point, as septic-pneumonia speedily follows unnoticed womb trouble and usually ends fatally. Some bitches are naturally so upset after whelping, that it takes them a few days to feed up readily, but I have never had a case in which womb trouble was not found to be the cause of a bitch going off her feed after once having come well on to it.

If the bitch feeds up well two days after commencing Osoko, she goes on to equal parts of Osoko and ordinary kibbled biscuits soaked in broth and with 1½ pints milk added to each feed, three times a day. The limewater is continued, and a dessert-spoonful of fish meal added to each feed. Up to about ½lb. raw meat a day is also given, either as a separate feed or mixed with the biscuit.

The quantity of Osoko is gradually diminished until it is entirely replaced by ordinary kibbled biscuit when the litter is from a fortnight to three weeks old.

So much for the mother : now for the children. At just over three weeks old the puppies get their first feed—about a half-teaspoonful each of scraped raw meat once a day. Three or four days later they are promoted to three feeds a day—an ounce of scraped raw meat to six puppies once a day and half a teacupful of warm (scalded) cows' milk or Lactol (not raw milk—it scours) to each puppy twice a day. Twenty per cent. of limewater is added to all milk feeds.

At four weeks a dessert-spoonful of Osoko per puppy, and a pinch of fish meal (a teaspoonful between three) are added to the milk feed and given well soaked.

At five weeks a small quantity of minced (cooked) meat is added to the Osoko, and the latter is now soaked in hot broth instead of milk. Three feeds are still given, but the puppies have two drinks of warm (scalded) milk (about half a teacupful each, with limewater as above) in addition.

Care must be taken not to let the puppies eat enough to cause distension.

The puppies may be entirely weaned at six weeks if the bitch's figure has to be considered from a show point of view, or if the puppies are unusually strong and worry her too much. But I prefer to let the bitch take her puppies at night for another week, especially in winter.

After weaning, the puppies are given five feeds a day. First feed, warm porridge and milk ; second, Osoko, or fine kibbled biscuit soaked with broth, and with an ounce of minced meat (cooked or raw) to every six puppies ; third, Osoko, soaked in warm milk ; fourth and fifth feeds as second. The puppies get a small drink of milk after their last feed. Twenty per cent. limewater is still given in all milk feeds, and the fish meal is slowly increased with each biscuit feed till at about nine weeks old the amount is about a dessertspoonful to every three puppies per feed.

This feeding is continued up to four months old, the quantities being gradually increased till the meat ration is about ¼lb. per head per diem.

Eggs are very beneficial from eight weeks onwards, and nothing gets the puppies into condition better. If expense is not a consideration, they may be started with one raw egg, increasing up to three per diem. But, personally, I must admit I only indulge puppies likely to become "fliers" in this manner.

I may mention here that I consider feeding large quantities of meat (especially raw meat) to young puppies increases their liability to fits during distemper. I know, however, this view is not universal.

After four months old the puppies go on to the ordinary feed of the big dogs, but are fed four times a day, and have a dessert-spoonful of fish meal with every feed. Three feeds a day at five months ; two at a year ; and, provided they are in good condition, one feed a day after eighteen months. But the number of feeds a day after four months is not rigid, and every individual dog has to be studied.

I invariably "worm" puppies at about two months old, and unless they have then proved to be clear—again at four months. The puppies are given a milk feed about 4 p.m., and starved until 9 a.m. next morning. They then get a puppy worm-pill, followed half an hour after by a dessert-spoonful of castor-oil and a drink of warm milk a quarter of an hour later. Especial care must be taken in cold weather that the puppies don't catch a chill after dosing, and a spell of mild weather should be chosen for "worming," even though it may delay the dose for a week or two.

As soon as weaned the puppies are encouraged to follow me in my work round the farm, and are introduced to the fowls and the pigs running in the fields. Their exercise does not exceed a quarter of a mile a day to begin with, and is preferably increased a few yards at a time several times a day, working up to two half-mile walks at nine weeks. Great care is necessary to see that they do not get over-tired. The first indication of this is the puppy allowing his knees to "give" forward and, if continually over-tired, he may develop this habit permanently.

At the same time, there is far more danger from under-
than from over-exercising, as the former usually causes weak
pasterns, weak hocks, and splay feet, particularly in a
heavy puppy.

At about four months old the puppies do from two to
four miles a day round the farm, and at five months they
start exercise with the horses, doing up to about six miles
at average paces.

The greatest care must be taken in the housing of puppies.
They should be on a dry wood floor, just raised off the ground
to permit an undercurrent of air, and with plenty of clean,
dry straw. Sawdust is used in cleaning out the kennels.
Wet concrete is as fatal to puppies as it is to pigs, and is a
great source of sickness.

I wish again to emphasize the advisability of giving fish
meal to in-whelp and suckling bitches, and to the subsequent
litter, when old enough to digest it. In my opinion it is
invaluable for supplying bone-forming material and vitamines,
which is so necessary to prevent rickets. It must, however,
be given with caution, as it is liable to cause scouring.

Milk should always be given scalded, otherwise it is liable
to scour puppies.

Every individual puppy must be watched when feeding,
and stopped immediately he begins to blow out. One of the
most serious faults is giving sloppy food to weaned puppies.
This is, in my opinion, a very common cause of rickets.
Sunlight, dry housing, and plenty of light exercise (a little
at a time) are—besides correct feeding—the greatest pre-
ventatives of rickets. Dark and damp housing, and lack of
freedom is asking for trouble.

Puppies should not be allowed to chew too many hard
bones. They overdevelop the jaw muscles and cause
" cheekiness." After eight months old (not much before,
especially with a heavy puppy) all dogs should be encouraged
to jump, and I firmly believe that if all Great Danes were
kept in real hard working condition, and made to jump
regularly, the " cripples " would very soon disappear from
our show rings. In the words of the immortal Mr. Jorrocks :
" No 'ocks, no 'unter ! " So also with Great Danes."

ROLF OF OUBOROUGH.

PRIMLEY ISABEL.

CHAPTER X.

Kennels and Exercise.

Kennels vary so much in construction, capacity, and price that a choice can really only be decided on by the owner's requirements and purse. If only one Great Dane is to be kept, it is not absolutely essential to have a kennel (though, I think, it is always advisable to have an outdoor kennel when possible), for Danes are easily taught, and seem to naturally have the cleanest of labits ; at all events, when I was in practice at Brighton, my house had no garden, but I always had one or two Great Danes. A kennel can easily be made to suit the owner's wishes by the local carpenter, or can be purchased for a moderate sum from any number of makers. It should always be large enough to allow the dog to turn round at full length, and its floor should always be two or three inches off the ground. It is a great mistake to keep a Great Dane chained up—it is inclined to make him savage for one reason—but if it is absolutely necessary, a stop-link spring should be fitted to counteract the effect of a sudden jerk, and there should be swivels to prevent the chain getting kinked. Even when this is done there is considerable risk of the dog's shoulders being pulled out of shape, and no really good dog, at all events, should be kept on a chain. Of course it may be absolutely necessary to keep him on a short chain, but when possible it is much better to have the dog on what I may call a running chain. When this is done, a wire rope is fixed between two trees or posts at a height of six feet, or fastened to two pegs firmly set in the ground ; on this rope is threaded a metal ring, and to it is fastened the free end of the dog's chain ; the dog can then move the whole length of the wire, for the ring travels down it as the dog moves. When there is only a kennel, and the dog is on a chain, the kennel should have a southern or south-western aspect, and it should be well sheltered from wind and rain. Trees afford shelter from sun, but they harbour moisture, which it is most important to avoid, and if there is nothing else an awning should be put up as a screen. It is infinitely better to have a small run made with iron hurdles which can be easily and cheaply purchased; the kennel and run can then be moved from place to place as it is little trouble to shift the hurdles. I find this plan most useful with very young puppies.

If there is a stable not in use, a loose box and stalls can be converted into the most excellent kennels at a very little cost, while, for those of more ambitious ideas, there are the big manufacturers who will provide you with any kind of kennel you fancy at a price proportionate to the size and style. I like to have a kennel house square, or nearly so, and measuring in its narrowest part at least as much as its occupant measures from nose to end of tail, while there should also be a covered run rather larger than the house. The floor should be of concrete, be fitted with wooden battens, which can be taken up, and Sanitas sawdust should be spread underneath these to absorb any moisture; it should also have a certain slope (for the purpose of cleaning), which should be continued in the run, which will, of course, also be floored with concrete. I say " of course " because it is advisable to have the whole of the flooring of the same material. Some people prefer asphalt, some stone flags, and others wood, but I think that concrete with wooden battens for both house and run is the best. The wooden battens enable puppies to use the run without getting cold, and they can be removed when the puppies are older and the concrete sprinkled with gravel. By doing this the puppies' feet are made cat-like, as they tighten up their toes to prevent the gravel getting between them. In the house itself there should be a movable bench, from six inches to a foot off the floor, a window, and proper ventilation. The main door should be divided in two, so that the lower half can be shut and the upper half open, and the exit to the run should have a door so that it can be closed if so desired. A kennel like this will do admirably for a bitch about to whelp, and will serve as a nursery afterwards, as with a few additions it should satisfy the most fastidious, though it is always advisable, when possible, to have a whelping bitch's quarters removed to some distance from the other kennels. Of course the bench must be removed if a bitch is to whelp in the kennel, and a bed of straw put down, as has been already mentioned. It is very nice if one can afford to have kennels warmed by hot water pipes, but when this is impossible a stove can be made to answer the same purpose. In this case it is advisable to have some sort of removable guard made to fit into one of the corners, behind which the stove or, if *in extremis*, a bucket of boiling water can be placed, and which will prevent the bitch coming too close. Some breeders like to have a low (about six inches high) removable wooden railing made to fit in the kennel at a distance of about six inches from the wall, after the fashion of that used in sties to prevent the sows lying flush against the wall, and so crushing their young. The six inches allows a puppy to lie between the bitch and the wall, but, though it is certainly an extra safeguard, I am not sure that it is really necessary, bitches being much more careful and sensible than sows.

When two (or more) kennels are adjoining one another, it is as well to have the partition separating the runs so made in its lower part that the inmates can be prevented seeing one another if it is desired. Sometimes, when they are quarrelsome or unfriendly, their proximity greatly increases their animosity.

I think that it would be an excellent thing, if it could be arranged, to have a screen made all round the lower part of the kennel which would prevent young dogs seeing anything unless they stretched their necks to see. I have never seen such a contrivance, but I do not see why a sort of blind, working upwards from the ground, could not be made, which could be raised to different heights as the puppies grew. It would be important, however, with this, as with the partition between adjoining kennels just mentioned, that there should be no shelf or ridge on which the dogs could rest their forefeet, as doing this tends to throw their shoulders out of position.

The blind that I suggest may appear a small thing, and perhaps a foolish idea to many, but anything that could be done to obtain the long snake neck, which should be a characteristic of the breed, would be greatly appreciated, I am sure, by everyone. Another important point of the same kind is that no puppy should be allowed to take its food from a plate or dish on the floor ; the food should always be on a level with, or slightly above, the dog's mouth. If the food is on the floor the puppies have to stoop down and spread out their legs, which in time produces a marked deformity of the shoulders. There are several methods of obtaining what is desired, the oldest and most primitive, but at the same time a very good one, being to place the dish of food on a couple of bricks, and to gradually raise it by adding more bricks. Another method is to have a framework of four legs, made with a series of holes in the legs, through which two iron pins can run to the opposite side and support the tray containing the food. The iron pins can be put through any of the holes, and so the height of the food can be varied at will. The chief objection to these two plans is that the puppy often places its fore legs on the tray and so injures its legs, though in a rather different way to when it bends down. The best way to avoid this difficulty is by a contrivance which was first brought to my notice by Mr. Blass, and of which a photograph is given. It is in use in the well-known Askania kennels, and I have since heard is universally used in the police kennels throughout Germany. In this method three or four large iron rings, each capable of holding a basin, are fastened to a narrow board, the ends of which have buttons which run in a groove of two uprights fastened to the wall ; the ends of the sliding board holding the basins can thus be fixed at any height by screws, and so the basins can gradually be raised as the puppies grow. The basins are so narrow that the puppies cannot possibly put their feet on them and eat at the same time, and they are thus obliged to stretch their necks to obtain their food. There is no doubt that feeding puppies like this helps to lengthen their necks, and anything that will do this is of the greatest value. The only improvement I can suggest on Mr. Blass' plan is that the basins should not be so close together. It seems to me

MR. P. BLASS'S DEVICE FOR FEEDING GREAT DANES.

HYPATIA OF HOLLYBROOK, HENGIST OF HOLLYBROOK, AND HESPERUS OF HOLLYBROOK.

possible that a dog might get each of its paws on a basin and so defeat the object of the raised basins ; if these were a yard apart it would be impossible.

As regards the dogs' beds the best straw is bad to beat, if there is plenty of it, while Elastene and peat moss are also excellent, especially the former, and one of these will certainly be all that is required. Peat moss becomes dusty and makes it almost impossible to keep the coat glossy and shiny. In any case it is of the greatest importance that the bedding, and the whole kennel should be absolutely dry, as rheumatism, which is most probably one of the chief causes of some of those slight and unexplained deformities that constantly occur, is caused by dampness more than anything else. Another important point to remember is that Great Danes are especially liable to kennel sores which are most disfiguring in a good dog. If there are any signs of these it will be as well to give the dogs cushions (made by stuffing sacks with wood shavings)* to lie on ; by doing this the kennel sores will greatly improve, and there will certainly not be any new ones. It should not be needful to say that the most perfect cleanliness in the kennels is absolutely essential. All basins and troughs for food should be removed directly the dog has had his meal, and they should be washed at once and boiled if necessary. The kennels themselves should be washed out every day with a disinfectant, the boards taken up and brushed and the floors washed, while fresh straw should be put in every two or three days. As to which disinfectant to use it would be invidious to select any one when so many are good. In addition to scrupulous cleanliness in the kennels and with the cooking, mincing, and feeding utensils, it cannot be too strongly impressed that the drinking water should be constantly renewed, and that it should be placed in such a position as to be completely sheltered from the sun.

" Reasonable exercise not only increases muscular strength but it also ensures symmetrical and properly balanced development, conduces to good nutrition and health, and greatly augments beneficial functional activities.†

Growing dogs, as a rule, require more exercise than those that are matured, but it behoves us to exercise the very

* Wood wool, hay, or Elastene are even better.
† R. E. Nicholas, " Kennel Encyclopædia," p. 603.

K

greatest care in exercising young puppies. Stud dogs and brood bitches must have liberty for ample exercise if they are to have healthy puppies. Overtaxing the energy of the breeding stock may not only weaken future puppies but is often a reason for non-conception. Many young Danes are often over-exercised ; because a dog wants to follow a cart or a bicycle it by no means follows that it is good for him to do so. The general condition of the dog is generally a fair guide as to whether the exercise is excessive or not. If a dog loses weight in spite of liberal feeding, it may be taken that he is having too much exercise, while, if he continues to gain in weight he is probably having too little.

Different breeders hold different opinions as to how Great Dane puppies (dogs up to a year old) should be exercised, and attribute various ailments or any unsoundness to what they consider the faulty method of exercising adopted by their *confreres.*

Personally, in rearing Great Dane puppies, I adopt the following method of exercising, and have done so for thirty years, and as I have had extremely few puppies go wrong in their legs, it must be something approaching the right method, or else I have been extremely lucky.

If the weather is fine, the puppies, when about four weeks old, are put with their mother in an enclosure (or run) in a field. Here they are weaned, the run being moved each week to a fresh place so that they are not living on soiled ground. At about ten weeks they are left free in the field, which has a large kennel or shelter in the centre, to which they can retire if the sun is too strong, or if it comes on to rain. They are now under no restraint and can run about to their heart's content, getting as much exercise as they require, and here they stay until they are eight or nine months old. I do not say we never take them out of the field, as we do occasionally take them for short walks, two or three hundred yards, but we do not make a rule of it. It is not often a puppy is shown before it is 8 or 9 months old, but if one is very forward, and is to be shown, it is taken out on a lead two or three times a day, to accustom it to the lead and to new sights. Still it spends its day in the field, only returning to the kennel at night. If one of the puppies is inclined to get splay feet,

which it may do if the ground is soft, it spends two or three
hours a day in a hard floored run which has been well sprinkled
with fine gravel, and this quickly puts the feet right. At
the age of eight or nine months they are taken for short walks
two or three times a day, which strengthens and hardens
their legs and feet, and does away with any nervousness,
though, if the field they have lived in adjoins the high road,
it is not often they suffer from this complaint. Nervousness
is indeed a real complaint, and I have known dogs the show
careers of which have been absolutely ruined by it, for they
sometimes never get over their fear of a new sensation and,
even when two and three years old, will cringe or run away
from a new sound or sight. Some fanciers think it very
important that the puppies when six months old should
be taken for a walk *on a lead*. They think that by so doing
the head can be kept up ; but I am sure that if the advice
I have given is followed it will be quite unnecessary to take
the dogs on a lead. The advantage of the method I adopt
is, I consider, that the puppies can have just as much
exercise as they want—if there are two or three there is no risk
of their not having enough,—and there is no danger of their
indulging too violently, which may quite possibly cause a
fractured leg or ruptured ligament. Personally, I think
that not only in their early puppyhood, but also throughout
their lives, this plan of turning them out is the best. It
is only when there are two or three stud dogs that it cannot
be followed, as they will be sure to fight, and in this case the
stud dogs must be exercised separately. I know two or
three kennels in the north where there are generally from
eight to fourteen, or more, animals (but only one stud dog),
and the plan answers admirably, as it does in other places,
for the Great Dane answers very readily to " pack law,"
and there is small risk of fighting. Of course it is not always
possible to carry out this plan—there may be no field or there
may be many other reasons to make it impossible. In these
cases the puppies must be exercised in the best way possible ;
if there is no other way the puppies must be taken for a
number of very short walks, as it must be remembered that
it is just as bad for puppies to have no exercise as it is to
have too much. In the former case, the joint between the

carpal bones and the radius and ulna (which is popularly known as the knee) gives way in the front legs, and the puppies walk on the carpal and meta-carpal bones. If this state has been existing for long it is almost impossible to get right, but if it has only been in existence for a short time, regular exercise on a hard road will put it right. It is a terrible thing to see a really good puppy in this condition, and I am sorry to say that I have seen it more than once owing to the owner being slack and not properly inspecting his dogs.

It must not be thought, however, that the method I advocate is the only one. There are many breeders who keep their puppies in their kennel runs, letting them out twice a day for an hour's exercise in a field. If this be done I think it best to take out as few as possible at one time, as by so doing there is less risk of the puppies hurting themselves. Some fanciers take their puppies on a lead when only five months—of course only for short walks,—and consider that the puppies benefit by it, while there is a well-known owner who always exercises her dogs by taking them with her when she rides ; she starts them at 3 months with a quarter of a mile walk twice a day, and gradually increases it until they do 5 miles at six months, and are then taken with a horse or bicycle, till by the time they are a year old they can do their twenty miles comfortably. I cannot think that any method of exercising which keeps the puppies in confinement the greater part of the day is good, and for this reason : the dogs are so excited when first let out that there is a great risk of their hurting themselves. A Great Dane puppy is not an animal of torpid or sluggish disposition ; he is as full of life as it is possible for a dog to be, and the way puppies of three to five months age tear about, knocking one another over, turning somersaults, even trying the " long arm balance " or any other gymnastic feat which enters the mind, if once seen, will not be readily forgotten. I feel sure that this kind of exercise is the principal cause of many of those mysterious deformities which arise, no one knows how, but most certainly exist.

It is of the greatest benefit to dogs, both adults and puppies over three months, that they should be well brushed and groomed every day. It is no light task to well brush and groom seven or eight dogs, but it is well repaid by the im-

GD. CH. REX LENDOR VON ZELTNERSCHLOSS OF OUBOROUGH.

Photo., *H. P. Robinson and Son, Redhill.*   CH. SANDRA OF LOOE.

proved general appearance and good health of the animals. Great Danes do not require to be washed except under exceptional circumstances; it is indeed a great mistake, combing and brushing being quite sufficient. If a dog has anything the matter with its skin, it is of course a different matter, and a washing may be required. In this connection I consider that a young Great Dane—and indeed the breed at any age—is rather liable to slight skin eruptions of an eczematous type. These irritations, which, though slight in themselves, give the utmost trouble if neglected, and perhaps necessitate the visits of a "vet." for several weeks.

After a dog is full grown it does not matter so much how he is exercised—whether he is turned out in a field or whether he is taken for a walk two or three times a day,—but on the whole I think the former, with a good road run two or three times a week, is the best. Some dogs require much more exercise than others, and I know one of the biggest and heaviest Great Danes, one who has achieved considerable success, who will gladly follow a carriage for twenty miles and be ready for another run on his return. One very important point about exercise is that the amount taken should never be suddenly changed. It might do a dog accustomed to a six or seven mile walk daily the greatest harm if he were suddenly taken for a twenty mile, and in the same way it is very inadvisable to suddenly stop a dog's exercise. There is a form of exercise—namely, jumping—which is one of the best for a Great Dane, and it is a great pity, in my opinion, that the jumping competitions which used to be held are not started again by one of the clubs which do so much for the breed. Young dogs should not be exercised by jumping; it is only after they are a year old that this form of exercise should be indulged in, as if started earlier a heavy puppy may easily damage itself in its legs or strain some of the muscles.

Distemper is unfortunately so frequently experienced during the rearing of puppies, and is so terribly fatal, that I consider it my duty to say something concerning it, and more especially so as I am informed on good evidence that there is a remedy which to all intents and purposes is a specific if properly used. I do not propose to say anything about the symptoms of Distemper—they are, unfortunately, too well known to most of us,—but I would insist that every case in the least suspicious should be regarded and treated as a case of distemper. I would go so far as to say that in young dogs, any case in which there is a rise of two degrees of temperature without obvious cause should be treated as distemper, and in the way I propose, as the treatment can do no possible harm if the drug is properly used. There is only one important point, and that is to watch the effect of the drug ; but as this should be done in all diseases and with all drugs it is no more than saying that the usual precautions should be taken. The drug I refer to is aspirin. I am perfectly well aware that if you ask an ordinary veterinary surgeon, or even one of the most experienced, whether he has used aspirin in distemper, he will reply, " Oh yes," and in answer to a question as to its efficacy, you will probably hear that " It is not much good." I can only say, with the greatest respect, that they have not used it properly. They have probably given five grains three times a day, or some such dose. Such treatment is absolutely futile ; the aspirin might as well be cast to the four winds for all the good it will do in curing or arresting the distemper. To have the result desired the aspirin must be given in big doses, and the patient must be got quickly under the influence of the drug. It is the same in the human subject ; no one would expect ipecacuanha to have its well-known effect on dysentery, or of salicylate of sodium to relieve rheumatic fever if the drugs were given in two or three grain doses ; and it is the same with aspirin in distemper. Directly there is any sign of the disease or any unaccounted for rise of temperature, a Great Dane of ten months should be given ten or twelve grains of aspirin (a dog of six months receiving eight or ten grains), and the temperature should be carefully noted. In about two or three hours the temperature should be again taken, when it will probably be found to be normal (101.4). This is very often the end of the attack, and the dog only requires careful nursing for a few days. If, however, the temperature is taken six hours after the first dose of aspirin, and *this should always be done*, the temperature will often be found to have again risen, in which case a second full dose of ten or twelve grains should be given if the pulse is all right. This will almost invariably terminate the acute symptoms, though I have very occasionally known a third dose required. I consider it most important to get the temperature down to normal, and keep it there in the early stage of the disease, as, if it can be done, it is very unlikely that there will be any complication such as pneumonia. It often happens that, as with measles in the human subject, a rash may appear,* and this I think should be encouraged, as if well developed the disease usually runs a mild and, I might say, normal course. The great guide in the administration of the drug is the temperature; while this is raised the aspirin should be repeated if the pulse is satisfactory. It may be thought I have laid stress on the condition of the heart, and I have done so because aspirin has a slightly lowering effect on this organ but personally I have never known the smallest ill effect from giving the drug in even larger doses than those here mentioned. In a case where the diagnosis is established without doubt the effect is practically the same, and I have never had to give more than three doses if the disease is treated before the third day. In a case where a dog has been ill for four or five days, and is possibly suffering from pneumonia, it is of course absurd to *expect* a cure; but I have known of some quite remarkable results, and I would always persevere with aspirin, even in what seems a hopeless case. It is, I imagine, hardly necessary for me to say that it is all important when giving aspirin to nurse the dog as carefully as if any other line of treatment were being followed. It should at the very onset of the disease have a jacket of gamgee wool sewn on round the chest and body; it should be kept in one room, which should be of an equable temperature, and it should be well and frequently fed with the most nourishing foods. If it refuses food it must be forcibly fed, but I have seldom found this necessary when aspirin has been used. I never give meat until the dog has appeared to be well for a fortnight, and then only in small quantities at first; but, on the other hand, I find meat juices and extracts of the greatest value. I cannot explain it, but I have found that of dogs suffering from distemper, a very large proportion die if they are given meat, while if only given extracts and

* I think the rash is always present, though it may be overlooked.

juices they recover. I know that many "vets." will disagree with me, but this is my experience, and I know of many other fanciers whose experience is the same. After the patient's temperature has been normal for a day, I start a tonic, such as quinine, strychnine, iron and phosphorus. The best form in which to give it is, I think, Easton's or Fellowe's syrup; half a teaspoonful twice or three times a day is the dose for a ten months Great Dane, and this may be increased to a teaspoonful twice a day. As distemper is an extremely lowering disease, it is essential during convalescence to restore the strength by the very best food, and plenty of it; as, moreover, dogs are extremely liable to a paralysis of the hindquarters after distemper—for what reason we cannot tell—it is most important that they should have the quietest time, with no exercise beyond what they take of their own free will. To maintain the condition of the muscles, which would otherwise very likely waste to some extent, it is most advisable that the legs should have a regular and thorough course of massage, and when this has been done I have never seen a sign of the weakness which is unfortunately so common, and has often ruined an otherwise good dog.

In the treatment of distemper by aspirin, I can offer no explanation of how it acts; I only know that it *does* act. The use of aspirin was first suggested to me by a doctor friend*—a man of very great experience both with human beings and dogs—who was struck, as I had been, by the close resemblance of influenza to distemper, and who had achieved great success in the former disease by the use of aspirin. I had used salicylate of soda with excellent results in 1894, when returning from Japan with some Toy Spaniels, and found its effect was wonderful, Aspirin is very much the same as salicylate of soda in its action, and as my friend has used aspirin in a great many cases of distemper, and on all kinds of dogs—Great Danes, Greyhounds, Bulldogs, Terriers and small dogs—it has caused me to give up the salicylate in favour of aspirin.

Veterinary surgeons may say that the treatment is empirical, and that they have used it, and it is "of not much use," but I can only reply that my friend and I have used it

* Dr. Osburne did not at first wish his name to be mentioned, but since writing the above I have obtained his permission.

to such an extent as to be absolutely satisfied as to its efficacy in curing and arresting the progress of distemper. I believe so absolutely in the drug that considering the enormous number of splendid puppies and dogs that die from distemper annually, I consider it my bounden duty to make known its use as widely and as quickly as possible. There is no serious disease that is more common amongst dogs, and none more fatal ; and I am sure that if people will only try aspirin in the early stages the mortality will be greatly decreased and the dreaded after effects be much more rarely seen.

I have somewhat modified my opinions from the above. What I have said in the previous pages was written when it was hoped that this book would be published in October, 1911. I had made extensive enquiries into the subject, and I thought it so important that the public should know everything possible. No harm could be done thereby, and there was a possibility of very great advantage. In the last six months I have been able to extend my investigations, and while I am sure that Aspirin is most valuable in certain cases, I could not designate it as a specific.

CHAPTER XI.

Character and Anecdotes.

Rawdon Lee, writing in 1893, says that he never considered the Great Dane a suitable companion or domestic dog. I can only say that I entirely disagree with him. If reared from its puppyhood by its owner I know of no dog more obedient, more intelligent or more companionable. They can be taught anything, as Rawdon Lee himself admits, for he says that one of the most wonderful examples of trick performing he ever saw was by some Great Danes who occupied the boards at the Oxford Music Hall in 1884. It was a very popular "turn," and I remember it well. Amongst other tricks which the "star" performer, a dog called Grandmaster accomplished, being a sham fight with another Dane. They are the most splendid house dogs, and if they live in the house they soon learn to efface themselves and take up less room than many dogs half their size. I will admit that the dogs of the 'eighties and 'nineties were a good deal more savage than those of the present day, but I think this was simply because they were not treated as companions. I, at all events, had no difficulty with them, and my experience seems to have coincided with that of other breeders who took a little trouble and made friends with their dogs, if one may judge from the expressions which I quote from Mr. Herbert Compton's book.* "There is no other breed of dog," writes Mrs. Horsfall, "to compare with the Great Dane as a companion for indoors or out. Anyone who has once had a typical Dane as a pet can never wish for a better. They are of huge size and awe-inspiring appearance, but when well trained and of good parentage are as docile and gentle

* "The Twentieth Century Dog," pp. 109-110.—Herbert Compton.

as could be wished, and delightful companions for lonely walks. In the house they are perfect ; if healthy and properly kept they are free from doggy smells, and soon learn to move about gently, and are not continually in a fidget like smaller dogs. They are grand guards too, being as sharp as terriers in this respect, and although good tempered will, when necessary, tackle anything required of them in an emergency." This character, coming from a breeder of the experience of Mrs. Horsfall, speaks volumes for the dog's nature, and other experienced fanciers all join in praising him. Mr. Hood Wright, for instance, writes, "They certainly require room, but in large houses they are capital house pets, being quiet, gentle, and dignified " ; while Mr. R. Miller, one of the original members of the Great Dane Club, and President of the Birmingham Great Dane Club, says "They have all the most desirable dog characteristics, namely, courage, gentleness, affection, reliability of temper, activity, strength, scent and intelligence." With all these remarks I entirely agree, and especially as regards the adaptability of a Great Dane to a small house. As we are now considering the Great Dane's character and his claims as a companion, it may not be out of place to mention those that were the constant associates of the late Prince Bismarck, of which Tyras was by far the best known. The following account is taken from the *Kennel Gazette*, and I think it certainly helps to give an insight to the character of the breed.

"Of all the dogs that have a place in history, Tyras, the noted realm dog of the German Chancellor, is the only one whose death has been deemed of sufficient interest to be cabled round the world as an event, not merely of European but of cosmopolitan interest. Indeed, the record of Tyras hardly ended with his life, for the cable has since told the world that the first visitor to Prince Bismarck on his recent birthday was the youthful emperor, who brought as a present another dog, of the type of the lamented Tyras. For nearly sixty years Prince Bismarck has owned specimens of the Great Dane, and generally has had one or more of unusual size. His first hound, acquired while living with his parents at Kniephof, was one of the largest ever seen, and was an object of awe to the peasantry of the district. This dog afterwards accompanied his young master to the college at Göttingen, where he speedily made his mark. Once when Bismarck was summoned to appear before the rector for throwing an empty bottle out of his window, he took with him his enormous hound, to the great dismay of the reverend dignitary, who promptly took refuge behind a high-backed chair, where he remained until the hound had been sent out of the room. Bismarck was fined five thalers for bringing this 'terrific beast' into the rector's sanctum, in addition to the punishment meted out to the original offence. As a law student and official at Berlin, during his travels in many lands, throughout his diplomatic career at Frankfort, St. Petersburg, Paris, and elsewhere, as well as at Varzin and at Friedrichsruh, Bismarck has always had the companionship of one or more of his favourite dogs. Probably the one to which he was most attached was Sultan, which died at Varzin in 1877. Tyras, who was of unusual size, and of the slate colour, which is most popular in Germany, was then quite a young dog, and he was the constant companion of his illustrious owner till the time of his death, sharing his walks, his rides, his business, and his meals, and keeping guard in his bedroom at night. Owing to his uncertain temper he was not often seen in the streets or gardens of Berlin. He was, indeed, regarded more as belonging to the 'Pomeranian Squire' side of the Prince's life than to his official establishment. At Varzin or Friedrichsruh, however, the two were inseparable. No sooner was the most absolutely necessary business of the morning dispatched, than the Reichskanzler sailed off with the 'Reichshund' at his heels, and for the rest of the day the long light coat and the battered felt hat of the famous statesman were not greater objects of interest than the huge dog which followed him everywhere, on horseback or on foot."

The mere fact that anyone holding such a position as did Bismarck, which involved constant intercourse with fresh people, should make a Great Dane his favourite companion is, I think, sufficient to dispel the idea that these dogs are naturally savage. If there be any lingering doubt in the mind of anyone as to their being suited for companions, I can only recommend him to try them.

CH. MAURICE OF CUDDINGTON.

Photo., C. F. Emery, Sudbury..

CH. ZARANE OF SUDBURY.

Although, as I have mentioned in the first chapter of this book, the Great Dane is supposed to date from time immemorial, there are no records of any celebrated personage in early times who made an especial companion of a Great Dane. The only person of note prior to the great Chancellor was a certain Lord Cadogan ; his Great Dane attended him during all the actions in which he fought under Marlborough, and their deeds are recorded in the tapestry of the seige of Bochain, which is now hanging at Blenheim.*

As regards stories and anecdotes of our hero, which most chroniclers of a breed are able to produce " thick as autumnal leaves in Vallombrosa," I am sorry to say that I have been able to find few that I consider authentic ; but whether it is because I have been careful only to take accounts the accuracy of which is beyond dispute, or whether our breed is so retiring that its great and good deeds are only done secretly—that they " do good by stealth," and would " blush to find it fame "—I cannot say. I incline, however, to the latter view, as the last four of the stories came under my personal observation, and I know the actors who figure in them well, and have done so for years.

E. Jesse, writing in 1846, tells of a Mr. Johnson who on a tour through Scotland with a Great Dane lost his way one night, but finally after wandering for some time came upon an old and lonely farmhouse. As it was quite dark he roused the inmates and asked for a night's shelter, which was refused him by an old woman who opened the door. Mr. Johnson insisted, however, as it was pouring with rain, and was finally told that if he would go and fetch some hay and litter from an outhouse he could stay. He consented to do this, but on its accomplishment was told that his dog could not come in the house. Again Mr. Johnson insisted, and as possession is nine points of the law, he and his Great Dane were finally shown into a large bedroom by the old woman. As he started to undress, Mr. Johnson noticed that his dog seemed very uneasy, and kept growling continually, particularly when he approached the bed. This was such an unusual occurrence that his owner decided to investigate matters, and commenced to pull the bed, which was a very

* The sketch which Mr. Dadd has made for me, by permission of the Duke of Marlborough, to whom I am greatly obliged, gives an excellent picture of the dog which will be found opposite page 5.

heavy old-fashioned one, out from the wall. As he did so, the old woman's husband, armed with a long knife, crept from under it, only to be at once pinned down by the Great Dane, who fortunately knocked the knife from out of the scoundrel's hand. Mr. Johnson at once joined in the fight, and with the aid of his dog was able to bind the man with strips of the sheet. Early the next morning captor and captured proceeded to the nearest town—Stirling, I think—and handed the man over to the authorities. After investigation it was found that several people had been murdered at the house, and it is probable that, but for his dog, Mr. Johnson would have shared the same fate.

There is another story told by Jesse, but while it goes far to prove the obedience of the dog, it does not say much for its intelligence, at least in my opinion. In this case a gamekeeper belonging to a castle of Holstein, after a long and fatiguing day's shooting, put some eleven brace of partridges and five grouse into the larder and told the dog, a Great Dane, which he had been using for his sport, to guard them. The door apparently blew to, or the keeper shut it inadvertently ; at all events, he thought no more of the matter that night, and the next morning was called away on urgent business. He did not return for five days, when, remembering the dog, he went straight to the larder. There he found the eleven brace of partridges, the five grouse, and a dead dog. Sooner than disobey his master the dog had starved himself to death.

A much more sensible dog was a Great Dane which was kept at a convent in France.

The brethren of the convent made it a rule to feed twenty paupers with a daily dinner, and the Great Dane made a special point of being present at the repast, as he always had a scrap or two thrown him, though they were few and far between, as the guests were poor and hungry, and naturally not very wasteful.

The Great Dane consequently had little more than a scent of the food on which he would have been only too glad to pass an expert's opinion, and as a result he set himself the task of evolving a plan which would at all events be personally satisfactory.

The portions were delivered by one of the brothers on the pulling of a bell rope, and were delivered by what in religious houses is termed a "tour," a contrivance like the section of a cask which, by turning on a pivot, exhibits whatever is placed in its concave side without discovering the person who moves it. One day the dog, apparently disgusted by the small quantity he had received, decided to try on his own account He waited till the paupers were all gone, and then taking the rope in his mouth rang the bell on his own account, and was promptly served. He repeated his tactics the next and every subsequent day until the cook finally noticed that while there were only twenty paupers on the list twenty-one dinners were given out. The brethren decided to discover the culprit, and a watch was set. The dog was observed to be lying in the court yard, and soon after the last pauper had received his portion he was seen to walk up and ring the bell, and to take the food from the "tour" when it was presented to him. I am glad to say that after a consultation had been held the brethren decided that he should be allowed a dinner regularly, and from that day it was a recognised custom that the dog should ring the bell and be served with his dinner. This story, which is vouched for as true, tends to show either that the dog could count up to twenty, or that he had sufficient intelligence to wait till no one had been for some time, and he could safely ring the bell without being seen.

Twenty seems a large number—too large—for a dog to count, but I am quite sure that some dogs can count, and I know one, a Great Dane, that certainly seemed able to count up to seven. I was taking care of her for a friend while she was whelping, and when her puppies were put back to her after they had been removed for the cleaning of the kennel, she always made the most terrible fuss if only six were put in. She smelled and carefully examined each pup as it was returned, and certainly seemed to know if one were missing. It was not any special puppy which she missed, as I tried all the puppies; moreover, two other people who tried the experiment noticed exactly the same behaviour on the bitch's part, though they were incredulous until they had tried it themselves.

The remaining four stories are of more recent date and are of much greater interest, at all events to me, as I knew the people concerned in all instances, and the dogs in two. The first happened to a well-known veterinary surgeon who was buying a practice. The purchase was completed, and he was visiting his new home for the last time prior to taking possession on the following day. My friend was talking to the vendor in the surgery when there was a scratching at the door, and on its being opened a large Dane was seen to be standing there. "Oh, it's that wretched dog again," exclaimed the vendor, and proceeded to "shoo" it away. "What is it all about?" asked my friend. "Well," said the other, "that dog has been down the last two days, it seems to have something wrong with one of its paws, but I don't know who it belongs to, and I cannot be bothered with it." The incident then closed, and my friend thought no more about it till the next day, after he had taken possession of the house, when at about the same time he was in the surgery and heard the same scratching. He opened the door, and there was the same Dane, who always came alone. My friend was better natured than his predecessor, and he brought the dog in and examined it. He found the leg broken and put it up in plaster. The dog came again several times, and finally the splint was taken off and the leg found to be sound. I regret to say that the dog subsequently showed no signs of gratitude, so that it points no moral in that respect; it does, however, show that the dog apparently knew that someone who could perhaps do him good resided in a certain place, and he made up his mind to go there.

I once met a Great Dane belonging to Mr. Kirwan, which, though it was not, I am sure, what he would consider a show specimen, it was remarkable for its intelligence. In addition to doing all the customary tricks, and many that are out of the ordinary, it was quite impossible to keep the dog in a room unless the door was locked. He would take the handle of any door in his mouth and turn it, as I have seen myself. It is easy to imagine the astonishment his appearance caused on more than one occasion after he had been shut up, not only in a room, but in a house which had its doors all shut securely.

CH. ZENA AND ZERO OF SUDBURY.

ZERO OF SUDBURY.

We frequently hear of dogs saving a household from fire, but I think that the following story which concerns Mr. Donisthorpe's Laird of Strathtay, popularly known as Jim, is much more remarkable. It is the custom for Jim to sleep downstairs in the house. When all the outside doors and windows have been shut, the doors of the drawing-room, dining-room, study, library, etc., are left open, and Jim has the run of the ground floor, and sleeps on a big rug in the hall. He never goes upstairs by any chance until after Mrs. Donisthorpe comes down to breakfast in the morning, when he immediately goes up to his master's dressing room. This is a routine performance. One night, a few weeks ago, after Mr. Donisthorpe had been in bed about an hour, he heard Jim come running upstairs. He called to him to go down, and he did so. About ten minutes after he came up again, and was told somewhat forcibly to go and lie down. He returned downstairs as he was told, but in five minutes he was up again and scratching at Mr. Donisthorpe's door. This time his master thought it was time to inquire into matters, and on entering the dining-room found that, though there was no light, the gas was fully on. We cannot help thinking this is a sign of a very great intelligence on the part of Jim, even greater than that of those dogs who wake their owners when there is a fire, as gas is a much less noticeable and terrifying thing than a case of fire. The dog, at all events, knew that there was something wrong, and also knew that if he went to his master he would put things right, as after Mr. Donisthorpe had rectified matters Jim laid down, and never went near his master until after Mrs. Donisthorpe came down to breakfast in the morning.

The last story is one of the most charming that I have ever heard as exemplifying the friendship which may exist between dogs, and how they will care for and help one another, the two chief actors being Great Dane bitches. The scene of action was some large and well-known kennels. The bitches were kept in a large yard, and adjoining and communicating with it were their houses, at the door of which their food was always placed in separate troughs. Now, two of the bitches had established a great friendship ; they were always together, and at dinner time the one who had finished her portion first always adjourned to the other's bowl and helped to clear it. Now, it so happened that one of the bitches, which I will call Alpha, had a very large appetite, while the other, to be known as Beta, had a very small one and ate very little, so that it was always Alpha who went over to Beta's kennel, where she was invariably made welcome to any food remaining. This custom and friendship of the dogs was well known to the kennelman, but as Beta, who was the better bitch, was doing satisfactorily, there seemed no reason to put a stop to the arrangement. After a time, however, it was found that the extra half ration that Alpha was having was beginning to affect her, and she was putting on flesh at an alarming rate. It was therefore decided not to allow her to have Beta's food, and to prevent her taking it she was chained up at each meal time, and kept on the chain until the bowls were removed. In spite of this it was found that Alpha grew fatter and fatter, while strange to say, Beta seemed to have developed an appetite, as her trough was always found empty. Beta, however, did not put on weight, although she appeared to eat twice as much as previously, and it seemed so odd, especially when taken with Alpha's increased corpulency, that the owner decided to watch. This he did, and to his surprise he found that directly the kennel-man had gone away, after putting down the food and chaining up Alpha to her kennel, Beta took up her trough of food and walked across to Alpha, with whom she had a pleasant meal, and no doubt laughed consumedly at the way they had tricked the kennelman. After the dinner was over Beta walked back with her empty trough, and no one would have ever guessed at such manœuvres if a watch had not been set. I don't think I have ever known a case where more intelligence was displayed by animals, or which supplied better evidence of the innate good-heartedness and friendship which may exist between them. It was sad that it was necessary to frustrate their carefully devised plans, but for the sake of their healths it was obligatory, and it is most satisfactory to know that it did not interfere with their friendship.

CHAPTER XII.

The Commoner Ailments of Great Danes.

By A. Cornish Bowden, M.R.C.V.S.

I have been asked to contribute a chapter to this work on the most common diseases peculiar to Great Danes. As far as I am aware there is no disease really peculiar to this breed, and since it has become so popular, nearly every complaint has been discussed and written about in the dog papers and journals, so that any general discussion appears superfluous. The complaints, however, which appear to cause most annoyance to their owners pertain to the ears and tails. We who keep Great Danes know well the experience we get when the walls, ceilings, and floors are liberally besprinkled with blood, and how, after bleeding has appeared to stop for a day, an extra joyous wag of the tail or shake undoes all we had flattered ourselves we had accomplished. We most of us have our little remedies and fetish for the trouble, all of which are successful to a greater or less degree, but the novice who first meets this most damaging and disagreeable occurrence may be glad of a few hints as to stopping it, or, at any rate, as to sparing further damage to wallpapers, ceilings, clothes, kennels, etc.

If we examine the ears of a great number of Danes on the show benches we are certain to find a large percentage with notches on the free borders, especially near the tip. The great majority of these have been ulcerating sores, caused and aggravated by the incessant shaking of the head, which bleed freely at the slightest provocation, scattering blood far and wide over everything near, quite irrespective of persons, paint, or wallpapers.

The first thing we must ask is what starts this constant shaking, and it should be noted that it is not so often the sores on the tips (which really arise from it), as irritation within the ears. There may be several causes for this, but I venture to think that the commonest is dirt.

There is a natural secretion of sebum (the name given to the wax) in the ears of all animals, added to which there is a certain amount of perspiration and moisture, especially found in such ears as are pendulous and hang down.

This moisture, whether waxy or sweaty, serves as a harbour for dirt and dust, which often causes the irritation which first starts the shaking. If Dane owners would only be a little more careful to clean the insides of the ears, I am sure they would save themselves an immense amount of trouble, and there would be fewer lamentations over the cessation of cropping. Without doubt it was on account of this failing connected with the pendulous ears of Great Danes that cropping was first so universally resorted to, and, no doubt, it was continued as a matter of course because it was thought to give the breed a smarter and cleaner look, to say nothing of its tendency to remove the undesirable loose skin from the throat and cheeks, which appears to be drawn up by the cicatrisation of the crop.

The ears may easily be cleaned, if done fairly regularly, with a little absorbent cotton wool, either on forceps or a stick, but care must be taken not to leave the wool or any part of it in the ear. Should the dirt appear hard and dry, or even ingrained with the skin, a little of the wool dipped in methylated spirit will soon remove it. I never advise water being used for this for reasons which I shall explain later ; but with spirit there is a fairly quick evaporation, which leaves the ears dry and sweet. If a powder is used after, as is the custom with some people, very little should be applied ; just dust the surfaces, as large collections of boracic acid or other powder, though harmless in themselves, act as a foreign body and cause further irritation.

Sometimes, however, this precaution has been neglected too long, and we find we have sores in the ears and on the edges of the convolutions ; these cause some pain when touched, and the tenderness caused by them gives rise to an

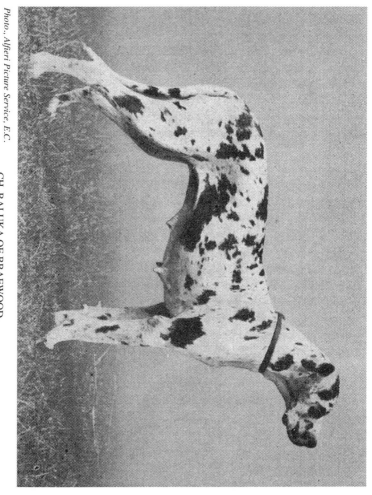

Photo., Alfieri Picture Service, E.C.

CH. RALUKA OF BRAEWOOD.

MICHAEL OF EVERLEY (AT 8 MONTHS OLD).

aggravation of the head shaking. If these sores do not heal up quickly, after the ears have been rendered clean, I think that professional advice should be sought, as in the vast majority of cases the bleeding ear tips will heal when you have removed the cause of the irritation inside. Oil poured into the ears causes a splendid medium for the growth of germs ; but if glycerine to which is added an alcoholic solution of a reliable antiseptic is used, it usually relieves the irritation, and if proper care is taken there should be no accompanying or after ill-effects and troubles. If the solution is used for a few days the results are wonderful, both inside and outside ; but it is essential to be careful to remobe the glycerine, which, like sebum, acts as an anchorage for dust and dirt.. It should always, when used, be swabbed out with cotton wool, and the ears wiped dry for several days afetr you have stopped using it.

If your stick or forceps are well protected at the tip with wool you need not fear penetrating deep down into the ear. The best entrance is in the lower part, as far forward as you can see in, then the direction is downwards and forwards ; the padded point of your instrument can next be brought backwards, and so clean out the whole channel of the external ear.

In the meantime we must do something to stop the bleeding at the tip of the flap. We know that if we could only keep it still the bleeding would stop, but to accomplish this we dare not use bandages, as the heat of the bandage only causes an irritating and sweaty condition inside. If anything in the way of binding is thought advisable, a net put loosely over the head is best. It must not be so tight as to bind the flap close to the head, as too much heat would thereby develop inside, but sufficiently tight to prevent movement, and at the same time allow far more ventilation than would a bandage. The nets that ladies used to use to carry parcels in were excellent for this purpose when cut to the desired size. In my experience they make an excellent pastime for the dog, who will spend many happy minutes trying to drag the net off, or in attempting to extricate his claws from the meshes. If the nets are not used as an amusement for the dog, someone should keep their eyes on him more or less continuously.

Many different applications are used for these ulcers, and I have been strongly recommended to try a red-hot iron; but though I know this is fairly freely used by some, I have never yet resorted to it, nor do I expect to do so. Even silver nitrate I have found too drastic and irritating for general use, and prefer to secure the formation of a hard adherent scab, under which the ulcer will heal, by the use of an antiseptic in combination with the sulphate of zinc of some such lotion. Powdered iodoform is excellent, especially if put on just before you start out for a walk or loosen your dogs to play, as at these times it is seldom interfered with.

Another cause of irritation in the ear which is of common occurrence is the presence of a parasite of a similar nature to the common parasites of mange. This parasite is known by many names, but perhaps the commonest is *Symbiotis auricularum*. This symbiot flourishes well in the presence of moisture and sweat, and it is on account of this that I never use water inside the ear, as however careful you may be to dry it, some of the moisture is certain to remain, and moisture is in every way suitable to promote the growth of the parasite, while if spirit is used this is not the case. The parasite causes intense irritation, which is chiefly indicated by scratching behind the bulb of the ears and by shaking the head; it is easily killed by the above-mentioned treatment or by any parasiticide, and is contagious to other dogs, spreading rapidly from one dog to another, but there is no evidence to show that the parasite can exist outside the ear of the dog.

Proceeding from one extremity to the other I fancy the tail is the next appendage which gives trouble to the beginner. Few there are who have kept Danes for any length of time that have not had experience of much the same sort of annoyance with their dogs' tails as I have just mentioned in connection with the ears. By reason of the constant knocking against extraneous objects and the dog's own sides we get a bleeding wound on the tip of the tail, which is excellently adapted to spread blood around any object within yards of the sufferer. Again, the tail is no respecter of persons, and, as a rule, when a dog suffering from this affliction meets his master, that master, at the first indication of pleasure, resembles a butcher, and if the meeting takes place in a house the walls are highly reminiscent of a slaughter-house.

If a tail, in this condition, is treated early, little damage is done, as a rule, but if the wound is in any way neglected, and the dog's tail is allowed to wag and strike the kennel walls or any object within reach, the wound at the end of the tail becomes an ulcerated mass, and we often get necrosis, or death of the bone, at the tip. This seldom or never heals unless the diseased bone is removed or the whole tail is shortened. A curious point to be mentioned in connection with this is the apparent total absence of pain. That the tail is well supplied with sensory nerves we know well, yet the dog will continue to dash this sore and bleeding tail against everything (including its own sides) with a recklessness that would indicate a complete absence of feeling.

If taken in hand early these sores are not usually hard to heal, but the trouble is that when there is only a small red spot little attention is bestowed on it. If at that time a little astringent antiseptic lotion were applied we should probably find that a scab would form that would stand quite a lot of knocking about. If, however, owing to the dog's excitability and "life," the movements of the tail are too frequent and violent it is an excellent thing to glue a pad to the tail an inch or two above the sore.

This pad is conveniently made with felt or cotton wool. If the former is used, cut the felt at first about four inches wide and glue it to the tail, then glue another layer to this, and so on until you have a cushion standing out about two inches from the hair. Cover this with a bandage, also glued on, and allow the whole to set and harden. When it is finished it will be found that there is a firm and sufficiently strong "buffer" to protect the sore when the tail meets the dog's sides or other extraneous objects, and thus gives the tip an opportunity to heal. When lying down this cushion also meets the ground, and the tip of the tail is no longer bruised, as even if he gets it under him, as is often the case, the pad prevents him exerting any pressure on it.

If cotton wool is used I also glue the tail and put on a layer of it ; then I take a turn with a bandage, gluing it, then some more cotton wool, and so on until a similar cushion is formed.

This can be left on until the tail is healed, and I have seldom found the dog is inclined to remove it ; dusting with iodoform, tannoform, or some similar preparation twice daily, is usually all that is required. If the tail does not heal even then, and there appears a small wound through the skin which is also inclined to discharge, we probably have a case of necrosis, and a surgeon's help should be sought. Even then it is seldom necessary to remove the tail, unless the skin has been hopelessly damaged ; it is usually possible to cut down on and remove the bone, leaving the skin more or less intact, and when healed there is little or no disfigurement left.

There is no doubt that these sore tails are often caused in the same way as bedsores, and are in fact bedsores on the tail. I have seen them in the process of being formed, and had one dog who appeared to acquire the habit of laying on its tail. Whenever it laid down, its tail came into the same position, curled around underneath it, and so, through constant pressure on one place, a sore was formed, probably mainly due to interference with the circulation of the part. A good pad soon broke him off the habit of lying on it, and the mischief rapidly rectified itself.

Bedsores on other parts of the body are a constant source of trouble. These occur chiefly on the elbows, hocks, and ischium, and are caused by the weight of the body pressing these parts against a hard substance, such as the ground, where they not only bruise the skin but stop the circulation of the part. They appear as bare patches, and chiefly on the parts mentioned, but may come in any situation* where the bone is practically immediately beneath the skin, and where pressure is brought to bear on it. The skin becomes thickened and regular callosities appear, from which, if the mischief is continued, we can usually squeeze a little pus, chiefly due to organisms that have been worked into the skin by the hard substance laid on. I have had considerable trouble with these, as although it is easy to give the dog a liberal bed, they often remove it all or work through the straw on to the boards or ground again. The best treatment I have found for these is either a mattress or a sack filled with straw and made to fit the bench on which the dog lies ; this he

* A well-known imported dog which had a very deep brisket developed one of these in the most prominent part of its chest in the centre line.

cannot shift, and usually takes to it kindly, regarding it, I believe, as a luxury. If this is done the sores soon go with the help of a little zinc ointment.

One other matter that I would like to mention as a warning to the novice, before closing this chapter, is the trouble we so often have with puppies' eyes. I have seen so much of this lately that I am afraid it is on the increase, and many a good puppy has been destroyed as blind or incurable when shortly after the eyes have opened it has been noticed that they appear weak or running or of an opaque blue colour. If the eyes are carefully examined it will often be found that the eyelashes are growing into the eyes or lie on them in a manner that is bound to make them sore through the irritation the lashes cause to the sensitive layers of the eye. This defect can always be remedied if they are treated in time by the surgeon. A small part of the lid bearing the offending lashes should be removed, when, during the process of healing, it will be found that the lashes are raised and no longer continue to irritate the eye. In bad cases this may need to be done more than once, but I have never yet seen a hopeless case if taken in hand before the eye is destroyed.

CHAPTER XIII.

Shows and Showing.

The matter of shows and showing hardly comes within the scope of this book, but as it is written in the main with a view of helping beginners, whom I hope may shortly become exhibitors, and as I have found that the majority of beginners are ignorant of any of the customs of showing, and even of the rules to be complied with, not to mention the routine of the business, I think I may be of assistance if I say a few words on the subject. It must be very annoying to be ignorant of what to do when wanting to show, and one may not care to ask, or even know anyone from whom to inquire, so that, although I know what I say can be found in other books and can be quickly learned by experience, I do not think this chapter will come altogether amiss to the majority of novices.

To begin with I should mention that all shows are held under the rule or sanction of the Kennel Club, and, though there is no Act of Parliament or Charter to give it authority, it enjoys such power as to control the exhibition of all dogs in the country. The Kennel Club possesses this power mainly owing to the goodwill of dog fanciers, who thoroughly appreciate all that the club has done for them not only in its administration of all the more important points of " dogdom," but also in its purification of the show-ring and supervision of the dealers, both amateur and professional. Years ago many people, with any regard for their reputation, were very shy of having anything to do with dog shows and dog dealers, and if the truth is told it must be admitted that they were right in so being.

The Kennel Club maintains its authority by disqualifying for life all dogs shown at an exhibition not under Kennel Club Rules, and by suspending from taking part in, or having any connection with, any show or field trial, for various periods of time, any person or persons who have been guilty in their opinion of discreditable conduct in connection with dogs or dog shows. The Kennel Club has delegated some of its powers to the Scottish Kennel Club, which, in its own area, exercises much the same power as the Kennel Club, but any show or private individual has the right of appeal on any point to the Kennel Club from the decision of any Club or Society to whom authority has been delegated. Supposing a person wishes to show his or her dog or dogs, the first thing to do is to procure a list of shows which are to be held. This can be found in the *Kennel Gazette* and *Our Dogs*. The name and address of the show secretary is always given in the *Kennel Gazette* (it can almost always be found in the advertisement columns of the other paper), and he should be written to and asked to forward a schedule when ready. This will contain a list of the classes, the name of the judge, and the amount of the entry fee, etc., etc., and it will be seen that it is absolutely necessary to register your dog at the Kennel Club. To do this, the owner should write to the secretary of the Kennel Club, 84, Piccadilly, W. 1, and ask for a registration form, which, on receipt, must be filled up and returned to the secretary with a fee of half-a-crown.

As to the information required for the registration, the most important points are the date of birth of the dog, the breeder, the sire, the dam, and whether these dogs have been previously registered, also the four grandparents. These can be ascertained from whomsoever the dog was bought, and if from any cause they are unobtainable, the words " not known " must be inserted in the space. All the other information required is quite simple. If the would-be exhibitor wishes to show a dog which he has bought, and which has been registered before (when purchasing a dog one should always ask if it is registered), he should write and ask the secretary of the Kennel Club for a transfer form, and on receiving it send it to the previous owner with a request that he will fill up that portion which relates to him ; then when it is returned to him he must fill up the remainder, and despatch it with the fee (5 shillings) to the Kennel Club secretary. It is customary for the vendor to send this transfer form, filled up, to the purchaser when the dog is bought, but it may, of course, be inadvertently omitted.

In which class or classes a dog should be entered depends largely on its merits, and a definition of all the different classes will be found in the schedule.

Having decided on the show and the classes, the next thing to do is to fill in the entry form, and this really presents no difficulty, a little care to ensure accuracy being all that is necessary. Only one dog can go in one line, but he can be entered in any number of classes, and it is not necessary to have a fresh line for each class, for the dog's name, date of birth, etc., are required to be written once only.

The one column which may present a difficulty is that which relates to price. The space should be left blank if it is not desired to sell the dog, but if a sale is desired the lowest amount acceptable should be stated.*

The entry fee for each class varies with the show, but it will be found mentioned in the schedule, and should be forwarded with the entry form to the secretary of the show. At some shows dogs of the same breed belonging to one owner are allowed to be benched together on the payment of a small fee, and this is a great advantage, as it enables him to look after his dogs and feed them with much less trouble, besides rendering the dogs' condition more congenial, as they will be much happier with their own familiar friends, besides having more room in which to move about.

It is most important that the fees should be sent off with the entry form, and it is advisable that both should go a few days before the date of the closing of the entries, which is clearly printed in the schedule, but it is all right as long as the envelope containing the entry form bears the date of the day of closing. Omission to enclose the fees may lead to disqualification of the dog, and it is useless to send forms

* Since writing the above I have while serving on the Shows Regulation Committee of the Kennel Club been struck by the enormous number of cases that are reported for inaccuracy in filling up forms. A dog is registered as the property of a lady and it often happens that her husband filling up an entrance form and thinking that as he pays for it the dog belongs to him, puts his own name as the owner. This is absolutely wrong and the *registered* owner's name must be given. Failure to do this leads to disqualification.

PRIMLEY QUINTUS.

PRIMLEY ISTRIA.

and fees after the day of closing, as they will not be accepted by the secretary; if they were accepted the secretary would be liable to severe punishment for infraction of Kennel Club Rules. It is as well to mention that receipts are not always sent by the show secretary, and to make sure of having one, a stamped addressed envelope should be enclosed with the entry form.

A few days before the show the exhibitor will receive an admission card, a metal tally, label, and removal order. The tally is to be attached to the dog's chain, and if more than one dog is being shown there will be a tally for each dog, with a number on it corresponding to that on the label and removal order. The admission order is transferable in case the owner should be unable to go. If no tickets are received two days before the show, the secretary should be notified that dogs are being sent or taken to the show, and it will save trouble if a card, with the name and address of the exhibitor on it, as well as the names of the dogs, and the classes in which they are entered, be sent with the dogs or handed to the gatekeeper on arrival.

If the owner or someone on his behalf does not take the dog it should be sent off in plenty of time, either muzzled and on a chain, or in a hamper. In either case the full carriage, including delivery at the show (this latter detail is most important, as railway companies often do not include the delivery charge, and the show secretary will then refuse it), should be paid in advance. Some people think that a Great Dane cannot be sent in a hamper because he is so large, but hampers are made large enough for any dog, and are much safer than a chain. The key of the hamper should of course be attached to it, and the name and address to which the dog is to be returned should be very clearly written on the label. If the regulation label is not sent, an ordinary one must be used, and on it must be written the name of the dog, with the classes in which he is entered, the consignee's and the sender's name and address. In whatever manner they are sent, the dogs should be despatched in plenty of time, and if there are two routes, the one chosen should be distinctly specified and written on the label, as if it is possible for the railway company to make a mistake they will be sure to do so. It is always better, however, to accompany one's dogs, and, personally, I should never dream of sending a dog of mine to a show unless I, or someone else went with it.

On arrival at the show the dog has to undergo a veterinary examination, and it will not be admitted to the hall and allowed to be benched until it has been passed. The examination is obviously of the greatest importance, and it cannot be too strongly impressed that it is a grievous offence to take a dog which is suffering from a contageous disease to any show. In spite of the harm they know they might cause. exhibitors, and often experienced exhibitors, frequently do it, and in my opinion they deserve the severest punishment for such behaviour. I think that it is almost criminal to do such a thing, and I look forward to a day when the Kennel Club may devise some means of making such exhibitors pay heavily for their disgraceful conduct. Apart from the harm they may do their own dogs, the mischief that may be wrought during the journey and at the entrance is incalculable, and I consider it is one of the most scurvy acts, an exhibitor can be guilty of. I would therefore advise any new fanciers, if they have any suspicion that a dog of theirs may be suffering from any infectious disease, not to hesitate for a moment, but at once to make up their mind not to show. It is very annoying to lose one's entrance fees, and I have two or three times experienced the feeling, but it is infinitely preferable, I imagine, to having a (perhaps) long useless journey and to seeing the disgusted faces of your acquaintances. It may be said by an exhibitor that he didn't know ; this, of course, is quite possible, but if I have seen the performance gone through by an exhibitor who DID know, who could have had no doubt, and who, after being refused at one door, tried to get in at another. Fortunately he was unsuccessful, as if he had been successful I should most certainly have reported the matter. Distemper and mange are the commonest diseases to cause a dog's refusal, but many veterinary surgeons consider eczema to be contagious, so that if your dog has only this disease it is better not to take him to a show. I may be thought to express. myself rather strongly on this subject, but it is a cruel thing that we cannot take our valuable and, far more important, often our favourite dog to a show without its running great risk of contracting distemper. Most people will admit that after one of the big shows it seldom happens that one does not hear of the death of some brilliant young dog and prominent prizewinner from distemper contracted at the show.

There is no real appeal from the veterinary surgeon, who is the show's official for the time being, though it is open to an exhibitor whose dog is refused to request the Kennel Club to inquire into the reasons which led to the refusal of his dog. If there are more than two veterinary surgeons in attendance, one of them may agree to act as referee, if there is a difference of opinion between the other two ; this, however, is very rare. If there is an objection to your or anyone's dog on veterinary grounds, the official veterinary surgeon's opinion is always considered, though it is competent for anyone to call in another veterinary surgeon for an independent opinion, and the same holds good for objections on the ground of " faking."

After passing the veterinary examination the first thing to be done is to bench your dog or dogs, and next to find out in what ring they will be judged and at approximately what time. It is useless to accept any statement made to you on this latter point, as the judge may change his mind as to the order in which he will take the classes, and it is well to keep in mind the fact that if your dog is on his bench the show authorities are responsible for its being shown, while they accept no responsibility if it is off. It is therefore as well, if you take your dog from its bench, to keep close to the judging ring so that you may know exactly what is going on. As regards behaviour in the judging ring itself I say nothing for the moment, beyond that the exhibitor should devote his, or her, whole time to the dog, and should on no account talk to any other exhibitor, ringsider, steward, or to the judge. When any particular dog or the class is finished with, the judge will notify the same, and at its conclusion the awards will be placed on the notice board. Besides the three (sometimes four) prizes that are generally given the following award cards are usually distributed : Reserve (R.), Very Highly Commended (V.H.C.), Highly Commended (H.C.), and Commended (C.). Special prizes are, as a rule, given immediately after the judging of the classes, and they may be confined to the members of certain clubs and societies, or they may be open to all. If a special prize is given for, say, the best puppy, confined to members of a club to which you belong, and you have won the second prize for puppies, you will, if the first prize winner is not a member of the club, be entitled to the special prize unless it is stated in the club rules or the schedule that only first prize winners are eligible. Special prizes are given under so many rules and regulations that it is impossible to make any definite statement about them, the awarding of each special prize being decided by the conditions under which it was given.

As regards removal of the dog from the show, if this is of more than one day's duration, a permit to remove for the night can be obtained on payment of £1 at the secretary's office. This will be refunded if the dog is in his place at the proper time on the following morning, but if not the money is liable to be forfeited. The dog can be removed for good at the final closing of the show, but facilities are generally granted for an earlier removal when there is a last train to be caught, though sometimes a small fee is charged even when early removal is really a necessity. A puppy can always be removed for good at the end of the first day of the show and without any payment; if, however, it is brought in on the second day for any reason it has to remain until the end of the show.

If an exhibitor or visitor to a show wishes to buy a dog which is for sale, he makes a claim at the secretary's office. Different shows have different rules, so that it is important that these should be read; it may be that the first person claiming it has it on paying the full amount. More often it happens that there is a rule that no dog can be bought before a certain time, and in such a case the would-be purchaser makes a deposit; there may be three or four more claimants, and then the dog is put up for auction amongst them and goes to the highest bidder, the show, of course, receiving a percentage of the money for which the dog was sold. If the owner of the dog thinks he has put too low or too high a price on the dog, he can alter it, or, if he changes his mind about selling it, he can claim it himself, though if there are

144

any other claimants he will have to bid against them at the auction; anyhow he will have to pay the percentage on its sale and the deposit if he claims it, and it should be remembered that a cheque will not be accepted unless the purchaser is known to the secretary, or the cheque is guaranteed by someone known to the secretary or one of the committee.

If you should wish to lodge an objection against any person or dog the Kennel Club Rules on the subject should be carefully studied. It is important to note that the objection should be lodged within 21 days of the closing of the show, and that there is often a deposit to be made which may be forfeited if the objection is considered frivolous. The rules of the various shows as to objections vary so much that one can make no *ex cathedra* statement, but it must be remembered they are only binding so long as they are not in opposition to the Kennel Club Rules, a copy of which is always to be found in the catalogue and schedule.

There are in showing many pitfalls for the beginner and snares of which he should beware, and though I cannot deal with many of these here, I may be able to help him in steering clear of some of the difficulties, and give him some advice which may be useful.

It is really impossible with dog fanciers to divide them into amateurs and professionals as is done in other branches of sport. I am aware that a distinction *is* made, but it is only because the professionals are honest enough to admit that they wish to make money by their dogs. There are certainly many so-called amateurs who make a great deal more money than does any professional, and while no one can object to a person selling his surplus dogs (for everyone does it), or of putting his best dogs at stud, it is a different thing for "amateurs"— and I am sorry to say that I think the majority of them are ladies—deliberately to lay themselves out to make money; one would at all events respect them more if they honestly admitted they were dealers. It must not be thought that I am writing of Great Dane fanciers only in making these remarks. I refer to the whole community, but I cannot help thinking that ladies are the worst offenders just as they are the sharpest, hardest, and I was going to say the most unscrupulous, in driving a bargain. I have known an amateur fancier who, when dealing with a novice who admitted that he was ignorant and asked for advice, not only demanded a most unconscionable price for the dogs sold, but deliberately glossed over their faults. If one goes to a dealer one does not expect him to point out a dog's faults any more than one expects a shopkeeper to run down his own goods, but from an amateur one expects the truth. Fortunately such practices do not pay in the long run, though they may succeed for a time, for fanciers such as I have described soon get known and people fight shy of them, and after a time will have nothing to do with them. It is far better to ask a fair price and even take a little less, and it is also much wiser to tell a beginner that the puppy he proposes to buy is not perfect, but has certain faults ; people will then respect you, recommend you, and probably write to you again if they want another dog. It is a good thing to make a rule never to send a dog out of your kennels that has anything the matter with it ; for this reason I always examine my dogs the day before they are to leave, and if there is anything the matter with them they don't go.

An exhibitor should never try to influence the appointment or the non-appointment (unless there is some very good reason) of a judge, but if the truth were told I think we should be surprised at the number of attempts that are made. If they are not successful these exhibitors will make a point of not showing, and, while they are perfectly entitled to take this course, they are not justified in persuading other exhibitors to refrain from taking their dogs, and this is what many of them do. Fortunately the majority of our judges are above suspicion, but it is most annoying that they should be made the victims of the underhand behaviour of others. We hear a great deal of the iniquity of the judges, especially from people who have never shown a dog, and hardly know a Great Dane from a Poodle; but, as I have already said, I think that, take them "for all in all," they are very honest. They have a very difficult and thankless task, and they usually perform it most carefully and most impartially. A man suspected of the unfairness of giving prizes to his friends, or of anything else not quite above board, soon meets with the treatment he deserves in small entries ; and, after all, exhibitors have the remedy in their own hand, for they need never show under such a judge. A resolution has been passed by the Kennel Club to prevent exhibitors showing a dog for a certain period when the person from whom it was bought or who bred the dog is judging.

It may be true that some judges are too prone to judge the wrong end of the lead, but they are not many, and I think it would be much more advantageous if exhibitors were to study their own behaviour instead of criticising the judge. There is far too much fault-finding with and cavilling at the judge's decisions, and too many audible remarks. The judge is, after all, human, and may make mistakes, but it is probable, or at all events possible, that he knows his subject better than the majority of his critics, who cannot help being prejudiced in favour of their own exhibits.

It is a great pity that so many exhibitors should display their feelings so openly at a show ; whether it is joy at victory or depression over defeat, they seem to find it a hopeless task to behave as they would ordinarily do in society. It is all very well to say " in the day of prosperity be joyful, but in the day of adversity consider." I certainly think that as regards dog shows, it would be better if exhibitors always considered. Some are such bad losers that they have no control of their temper; others behave as if they were absolutely ruined and their only hope was the poorhouse ; while others again go so far as to accuse the judge of par- tiality. It is no good saying such cases do not occur, as I have seen them, and though they are not often as bad as this, there can be no exhibitor of experience who has not seen examples of both ladies and gentlemen behaving in the most unseemly manner when suffering the bitterness of defeat. Almost worse I think are the people who are so disgustingly elated as to make the ringside unbearable though they may have won with nothing better than a third-rate dog. The man who keeps cool in the hour of victory, and who does not run other people's dogs down when he is on the losing side, will generally be found to be the most popular exhibitor, and it will generally be found that he will do all he can to help

N

the beginner and to put him in the right way of doing things, even though it is at considerable inconvenience to himself.

There are several things to which it would be well for the beginner to pay attention, and consider both before the show and when he is in the ring. In the first place, having decided to show, he should see that his dog is in the best possible condition he can bring it to, and even though, as I trust, it has been always kept in good form, he should try to improve this during the month previous to the show by regular grooming, exercise, and the most constant attention to everything in connection with the dog and its health. If it is a young dog that is to be exhibited it should be carefully taught the use of a collar and lead for at least six weeks before it goes to the show. There is nothing more trying for a judge than to have a dog brought in on a lead to which he is not accustomed, and which causes him to struggle, fight, and be dragged round the ring in a sitting posture, simply because his owner has not taken the trouble to give a little instruction beforehand. It is not at all difficult to teach a dog the meaning of the lead if it is always put on at meal times, and apart from saving the judge from being annoyed, a dog cannot show himself properly when he is struggling against the lead, and often loses a place in the money from this cause alone. Another lesson a dog must learn before being taken to a show is not to be afraid of noise or a crowd ; many young dogs cower down when placed in the ring, will not move at all, and at once throw away any chance they may have of winning. The best way to start this lesson after the dog has been taken out in a fairly crowded street is to take him to a big railway station for half an hour every day on a lead. There he should be fed, and if this is done it will generally be found that before long he pays no attention whatever to the noise. Occasionally I have found a little difficulty in getting a very timid dog to eat at first, but if this happens I take him into the refreshment room, where he will seldom be found to refuse a saucer of milk. The last and perhaps the most important lesson for the dog to learn before going to a show is to stand properly and display his points to the greatest advantage. There are some dogs that have been taught to absolutely " ask " for a prize—they stand so splendidly, with only the slightest lead, or even none at all. This is not at all a difficult thing to teach, most dogs learning it very quickly, and it makes the greatest difference to a dog's appearance, besides helping the judge. There are some people, mostly ladies, but not all (for I know one man who has a bitch that stands like a graven image), who have brought their dogs to a state of perfection as regards their behaviour in the ring ; it is a lesson, moreover, that is well worth teaching, for I am quite sure it has just made the necessary difference in the winning of many a prize. Mrs. Horsfall was wonderful in what she could make her dogs do, but there are ladies of the ring to-day who would make formidable rivals even for her, and it is a pity that there are not more. In contradistinction to this teaching of a dog to stand naturally, if I may so call it, I would impress on beginners to do nothing by physical or artificial means to make a dog show his good points or hide his bad ones. Don't for pity's sake, put the collar on as high up as possible under the jaw-bone, and haul upwards in a vertical line for all you are worth. This may make the dog look as if he had a fine long neck, and may hide the loose skin of the neck, the dewlap, but any judge worthy of the name will ask you not to hang your dog ; and, on releasing it, the difference in the dog's neck, with its loose folds of skin, will be far more marked, and probably have a far greater influence on the judge's mind than if he had seen it in its natural condition in the first place. Another thing which it is very foolish to do is to hold the dog's ears over his head or to spend your time in the ring in placing the ears in the position they would occupy if cropped. Both practices are ostensibly for the purpose of showing the beautiful "long clean chiselled head," but as a matter of fact they are usually really done to draw attention from big ungainly ears.

Don't be late at a show, as it may necessitate your taking your dog straight from his travelling box to the ring, in which case he is likely to cause unpleasantness and is certain not to show as well as he is capable of doing.

The best thing to do, having arrived in the ring, is to get your dog to stand in position, and to remain perfectly quiet yourself until asked to move. It is not advisable, if

You are in the first class to go in too soon, as if you do you will probably have to wait at least ten minutes, which is tiring for your dog ; as long as you are close to the ring, and ready to enter when required, it is all that is necessary, and your dog will not be tiring himself. It is as well to have a good long lead, not so that your dog may wander about and get entangled with the judge's legs, thereby attracting his attention, which I am told is a favourite device of Fox-terrier fanciers, but because the dog shows himself off better when standing alone.* Keep your whole attention fixed on your dog, and remember that while it is the judge's business to find the faults in the dogs, it is for you to try to conceal them, though, as I have already pointed out, an over-anxiety to do this on your part will often defeat its object.

When walking your dog round the ring be sure to keep on the outside, otherwise you are between the judge and your dog—and so hiding him. Never talk to any other exhibitor or any ringsider, as your conversation will only tend to distract the judge. Never speak to the stewards in the ring unless previously addressed by them, and, above all, however well you may know him, never speak to the judge, as the other exhibitors will only think you are trying to take an unfair advantage of them. It should be a cardinal rule for a judge never to speak to an exhibitor in the ring, and if he wants any information about a dog he can obtain it through his ring steward.

If one of the other dogs in the ring appears savage and anxious to fight your dog, avoid its locality as you would a pestilence, for however obviously it may be the other dog's fault, its owner will be sure to say that your dog irritated it. If it is feasible it is best to move to the other side of the ring, but if not make a point of interposing yourself between the two dogs. I have known in past times the most unpleasant contretemps owing to ill-tempered dogs, and even at the present moment there is, I believe, a family feud between two well-known champions.

* Of course if I were a beautiful woman, and a man was judging, I might do otherwise ; but, with the majority of judges, even under such circumstances, it will be found better to act as advised in the text.

Never take squeakers, talking dolls, artificial rabbits, or any live animal into the ring, with a view to making your dog look alert. He ought to do it when you call him. All such artificial aids, and especially the bobbing about like a jack in the box of your kennel-man or kennel-maid, and the uttering of strange unearthly noises from unexpected places, must be most annoying to the judge; though they should not affect his judgment, it is not as a rule so satisfactory to be judged by a man who has been recently irritated as it is by a man who is at peace with all the world.

If you use whitening or any preparation for cleaning your harlequin's coat be sure to have it all thoroughly brushed out before going into the ring; there are always people ready to make spiteful remarks and to make objections.

Don't visit the kennels of anyone with a view to purchasing a dog two or three weeks before you propose showing under him.

Don't write to a judge and ask him if he attaches very much importance to colour, or any other question if it can be deferred for a time.

Don't take dogs entered " not for competition " into the ring; the stewards have usually enough to do without asking you to remove them.

If you are sitting round the ring don't remark in a loud voice that you know the judge will give the first prize to " so-and-so," as he always favours that colour or always does something else.

Don't criticise other exhibitors' dogs in a loud voice, and don't make audible personal remarks about their owners, both of which seem favourite amusements at dog shows. Don't make excuses because you are beaten; different judges hold different views, and however good your dog, you are sure, sooner or later, to come across one who prefers another dog.

Don't ever sell a dog or a puppy if you know that it has anything the matter with it, and if you should in ignorance sell one, do all that you can to meet the person who has bought it. If you should have such a dog or puppy sold to you don't immediately write to the vendor accusing him of disgraceful conduct and saying you will return the animal at once. Remember that it is not to the interest of a respectable

151

person to sell an unsound dog, that it is probably no fault of his, and that he will be just as annoyed as you yourself are.

In advertising your stud dog don't boast and proclaim that your dog is " everywhere admitted to be " or " is without question " the best dog of his colour. Some one may question the fact, and you will look somewhat foolish if you have to climb down, or if you are challenged to a match, and you are so afraid of being beaten that you have to make some excuse.

Lastly, before dealing with the judge, I would say do not when in the ring call your dog by his registered name when he has a kennel name by which you always call him, and by which he is well known to your friends. If you are fortunate enough to possess a champion registered as Tommy Burns, but who rejoices in the kennel name of, and you always call " Jack," it is hardly good form to keep saying "Come here, Tommy Burns," "Lie down, Tommy Burns," especially if you are showing the dog under a judge who has never seen him before.

If, after he has been showing and breeding Great Danes for some time, a fancier is one day asked to officiate as judge, he should, provided he feels competent, accept. Though a great honour it is not altogether a pleasant task, especially on the first occasion, but it is one that everyone should help in and do his share of. Moreover, a fellow-feeling makes us wondrous kind, and after judging at one or two shows anyone will be much more chary of criticising the judge, as he will realise the difficulty of the work that has to be done.

It is best not to go near the benches when judging, and do not on any account look at a catalogue. There is no real harm in it, but the beginner will very likely think that it is done to find out the numbers of the best dogs or of friends' dogs. It is best to do nothing that can possibly give rise to unkind remarks.

Study the convenience of the exhibitors; they are honouring you by showing, and in common courtesy you should consider their wishes as far as possible.

Don't try to identify any dog that comes before you in the ring ; you will probably judge them better if you can dismiss all previous knowledge of the dogs and their records from your mind.

Allow exhibitors every possible chance of showing off their dogs ; give them every latitude, as while it is your object to find out all the dogs' faults, you wish, at the same time, to see them at their best.

Don't be hurried into awarding the special prizes at your stewards' suggestion that they follow the class awards ; though many of them do so, it will usually be found that some do not, and that the wording under which they are awarded wants to be carefully studied. Don't allow the exhibitors to crowd round you either when awarding the specials or measuring for the biggest dog present ; it is a favourite pastime for them—but most inconvenient.

Don't, on any account, place two dogs equal first—one is always better than the other : it is a sign of weakness and a disinclination to commit yourself to a definite opinion, which is the one thing you are present for.

Don't enter into a discussion with any of the exhibitors, as it will only give rise to ill-natured comment ; don't enter into conversation with a ringsider, as it is not polite to the exhibitors who are thereby kept waiting.

Don't give any explanation of your placings, at all events at the show.

Don't judge by one point, but consider the general appearance and all-round excellence.

Sort out and dismiss the worst dogs, as it will save time ; but while you do not wish to waste time, or take an excessive time, remember that you are asked there to find out the best dogs, and that if you cannot make up your mind in half an hour, everyone would prefer you taking an hour than giving a hurried decision.

Remember that if you satisfy yourself in your judging you have done your best, and you can do no more ; lastly,

> " To thine own self be true,
> And it must follow, as the night the day,
> Thou canst not then be false to any man."

Lightning Source UK Ltd.
Milton Keynes UK
UKHW012359180522
403146UK00002B/72